History of Texas

A Captivating Guide to Texas History, Starting from the Arrival of the Spanish Conquistadors in North America through the Texas Revolution to the Present

Free Bonus from Captivating History
(Available for a Limited time)

Hi History Lovers!

Now you have a chance to join our exclusive history list so you can get your first history ebook for free as well as discounts and a potential to get more history books for free! Simply visit the link below to join.

Captivatinghistory.com/ebook

Also, make sure to follow us on Facebook, Twitter and Youtube by searching for Captivating History.

Contents

Introduction

Texas is one of the most recognizable states in the United States of America (it is the second-largest, behind Alaska), and it also has a reputation for being unlike any other. This reputation is well-deserved, in part because of the state's long and often contentious history. That history has fascinated many people not only in this nation but around the world for centuries. From the heyday of the Wild West and the state's oil boom to the storied Texas Rangers and the construction of one of NASA's primary facilities, it seems nearly impossible to fully explore everything in the state's rich past.

While the real history isn't nearly as well-known as the stereotypical images of Texas, the state has a past that dates back millennia before the arrival of Europeans in North America. The native peoples had a diverse range of cultures and beliefs – much more diverse than the few religions practiced in Europe. These original inhabitants adapted to the different environments in the vast areas of the state, carving out existences with knowledge and rituals that have largely been lost to time and the arrival of the Europeans. Even the name "Texas" derives from a Native American term that was adopted by the Spanish as they started to persecute and displace the native peoples.

The Spanish and French were the first Europeans to explore the expansive lands. Their arrival initiated the first major shift in the genetic makeup of the region's population, setting the stage for several centuries of struggle as newcomers sought to take control of the native people's lands. Texas was always a highly desirable region due to its many natural resources and limitless potential. For several centuries, it served as a fertile place for cattle ranches, cotton farms, oil fields, and as a source of timber.

Both the Spanish and the Mexicans recognized how valuable the territory could be, but neither country had enough people to settle the region. The solution seemed obvious: they invited Americans to move into the territory and settle it. Of course, this invitation came with several stipulations, including one that required the Americans to give up their citizenship and trade primarily with Mexico. The chief problem was that the invitation to settle the region was extended while Mexico was fighting Spain for their independence. This decade-long war would affect the relationship between the settlers and the newly-forming country of Mexico.

There would be many contentious points between the American settlers and Mexico, two of the biggest being slavery and the unstoppable flow of new settlers rushing into the territory. The settlers had also largely been responsible for their own protection against Native Americans and bandits who prowled the countryside, which left the homesteaders with no sense of connection or mutual interest with their host nation. Over time, yearning for total autonomy ended in revolt, and the territory of Texas became independent. For nearly a decade, Texas was its own nation. However, many of the people living there had American roots and were struggling to get their new country admitted into the US—a risky move that would almost certainly result in war between the US and Mexico.

When the US finally agreed to annex Texas, American politicians had already formed a plan to ensure the acquisition of even more land from Mexico. Mexico was a new nation, while the US had been an independent nation for more than half a century and had built a robust military. However, the annexation of Texas ultimately became one of the causes of the American Civil War. Though it was still a new state, Texas seceded with the rest of the slaveholding states. This proved to be the one war that the intrepid Texans would not win.

Texas recovered relatively quickly, however, from the devastation of so much fighting, largely due to the many highly desirable resources available in its vast territory.

Texas is also home to some of the nation's most infamous criminals and has some of the most notorious settings from the Wild West era. For many years, Texas seemed to be immune to the law and order that characterized other parts of the nation, and that lawlessness gave rise to some of the nation's most intriguing historical figures.

Though it continued to have an economy based on cotton, lumber, oil, and ranching right up until World War II, there was still untapped potential for more. This potential would not escape notice by American leaders as the Cold War started to significantly shift the relationship between the US and other nations, particularly the Soviet Union. Houston became one of the most well-known cities in Texas when it was chosen to be home to NASA's Manned Spacecraft Center. This facility was instrumental in the early development of NASA and the space program, especially as the US and USSR engaged in the space race.

Today, the Texas economy is based on a range of different industries, particularly tourism. The extensive history of this unique state leaves little mystery as to why it attracts so much attention globally. Millions of people visit every year for many different reasons. Whether they want to see Fort Worth and the Alamo, visit the hip city of Austin, or attend space camp, there are a myriad of things to see and do in this vast landscape. If Texas were to successfully become its own nation again, it would rank 10th among the international economies in the world.

Chapter 1 – Before Columbus

Much of the history of the Americas taught in schools today focuses on how life changed following the arrival of Europeans. When Columbus first made landfall and the conquistadors began to explore the territory, all the land now known as Texas already had an ancient history filled with various rich cultures. While much of this history was lost because it was largely kept through oral traditions (much like the stories of Gilgamesh and other European tales prior to the rise of Rome), there are still many stories that have managed to survive the exploitation and genocide committed against the indigenous people in North America.

Often, Native Americans are lumped together as a homogenous group and thought of as similar in culture and religion. This is erroneous. Just as the people of Europe cannot be thrown together into a single category, thinking of all indigenous nations in the Americas as a monolith is an incredibly inaccurate depiction of what any of these people and cultures were like. North America is much larger than Europe; therefore, there was greater diversity among the Native American nations than among European countries during the 15th and 16th centuries. With the diverse environments in Texas, there was a wealth of different tribes with a wide range of cultures that had existed for centuries before the Spanish and Portuguese began to explore the land.

The Caddo and the Origin of the Name "Texas"

One of the most remarkable tribes that the Spanish encountered were the Caddo. It was from the Caddo language that the region would eventually derive its name. When the Spanish spoke with the native peoples, the Caddo used the term "tashya," which meant ally or friend. The Spanish would eventually spell the word "tejas" or "texas" (pronounced tay-hass), which would be changed to Texas in English.

The Caddo people largely made their home between the Red River and Eastern Texas, though they had originally lived in an area that covered what is today the states of Arkansas, Louisiana, and Oklahoma. Their homes were spread over a large portion of the northeastern part of Texas, and they were divided into twenty-five groups. These groups not only shared a language (Caddo) and customs but were also held together by a large confederation called the Hasinai alliance. Their customs and traditions were well established, and by the arrival of the Spanish and later the French, they would be respected for both their military prowess and artisanal skills.

What intrigued the Spanish and French most seemed to be how adept the Caddo were at trading. They did not differentiate between the different European groups (as the European groups did not differentiate between the many different Native American tribes). Spain and France eventually fought each other for the Caddo lands, and both wanted the Caddo on their side, which put the people in the Hasinai alliance in a precarious position. While they established trade with many other native peoples, this courting by the Spanish and French meant that a higher percentage of Europeans and their goods would flow through the Caddo lands. European illnesses would eventually kill as much as 95% of the Caddo people. The remaining people would eventually move to what today is Caddo County, Oklahoma.

The Fierce Apaches

Perhaps the most recognizable tribe in Texas were the Apache, an indigenous people that earned a reputation for being ferocious and fierce warriors who were far less inclined to simply accept the Europeans when they arrived. The term "Apache" includes many sub-nations, with the two largest groups in Texas being the Lipan and Mescalero. The name by which they are known today came from the Zuni language. In that language, "apachu" means enemy. Alternatively, the name could have come from the word "Awa'tehe" from the Ute language, although most sources cite the Zuni word.

The Apache gained their reputation for being fierce in battle in part because of their skills on horseback. They were the first people to acquire and use horses from the Spanish, and horses allowed them to travel much more quickly and easily. With the taming of horses, they began to live a more nomadic life than some of the other tribes in the region, which in turn allowed them to expand their trade and reach the southern part of the US. It is the use of horses as part of their regular lives that helped to make this one tribe such a familiar name in American history and lore. They traded with tribes in much more distant lands than their neighbors could, even acquiring obsidian and shells from as far away as the Pacific coast.

The Apache's culture and social structures were family-based. Males were always the leaders of the tribes, while the women shaped the tribal way of life. The men moved in with their wives after marriage, becoming members of the wife's family, even if she preceded him in death. When a wife died before her husband, her family would often help to find their son-in-law a new wife.

Hunting buffalo was one of the primary activities of the men, and tribes tended to follow the buffalo herds. Until the end of the 17th century, this was done on foot, but with the arrival of horses, the Apache could travel much further after their prey.

They were not always the fierce warriors they were portrayed to be. When the Spanish arrived and wanted to build missions, the Apache eventually agreed to help. The Lipan Apache helped to build missions and farm the land, although they largely ignored the attempts of the missionaries to convert them to Roman Catholicism. In return, the Spanish helped protect the Lipan Apache from the Comanche and Kiowa tribes. However, when the missionaries realized that the native people were still practicing their own religions, the tensions between the two groups began to grow. The missionaries began to demand more work from the Apaches and increasingly insisted they convert to Christianity. As the demands grew, the Lipan Apache eventually made the decision to leave the area. This decision was further reinforced by the missionaries' inability to supply enough food to meet the needs of the Apache, considering the amount of work that was required of them daily. Consequently, the Apache left and spread further west across Texas and Mexico.

The Comanche

The Comanche had an empire that spanned across a large swath of modern-day Texas. It is thought that they originally came from a region in Wyoming near the Platte River and had once been a part of the Eastern Shoshone. It is uncertain when they migrated south, but they formed their own tribe and, over time, gained control over a large part of the Texas region. They were one of the primary tribes in the north by the time the Spanish arrived. Shoshone who wanted to leave would often join the Comanche, growing the tribe over time.

As with the Apache, hunting bison was a large part of the Comanche's lives, and they were adept at hunting. The Comanche were more aggressive than many of the other local tribes, and it is generally thought that they stopped the Spanish from expanding further north. Like the Apache, they were skilled on horseback and knew the expansive landscape well, which made them incredibly difficult to fight. The Comanche took captives, and what befell those captives largely varied based on gender and the situation in which they were taken. Women would often be incorporated into the tribe and married off to the warriors. Many captives of both genders were often enslaved for a few years, if not for the rest of their lives.

Unlike other tribes in the region, Comanche formed no single nation or alliance. Instead, they were divided into independent groups that had the same culture and language. They would sometimes fight amongst themselves, but they largely focused on attacking their neighbors. While the Caddo, Apache, and other tribes had skilled craftspeople, the Comanche preferred to steal crafted items instead of making them.

The Comanche would prove to be the single most dangerous tribe to Americans who settled in or near their lands. Unlike many of the other tribes, the Comanche were not as accepting of the colonizers who invaded their lands and constantly fought to push them back east. The Comanche certainly earned their reputation as ferocious warriors, but the reason for their ferocity is understandable. The Comanche never agreed to any of the European colonizers attempting to lay claim to their lands, and the Americans were the first to try to steal their lands outright and settle on them, which precipitated many fierce battles. Like the Caddo, it was ultimately the arrival of European illnesses that would decimate their numbers. With their numbers reduced to just around 7,000 and many of those already on reservations by the 1870s, they could no longer fight for their lands. During the decade of the 1870s-1880s, the remaining Comanche people were moved onto reservations away from their tribal homelands.

Chapter 2 – Early Colonizers – Spain and France

When Columbus reached the Caribbean islands in 1492, it was only a matter of time before European nations came to explore "new" lands that they considered to be unowned. The Spanish were the first to arrive in Texas, but the French also explored the area in the coming years. The two nations would eventually fight over who would have control of this rich territory. It became one of many places where the European imperial rivalries would result in bloody battles.

The international fight between Spain and France would play out at the end of the 17th century. While Spain had arrived much earlier than France, France claimed a much larger portion of the continent. Both felt that the land belonged to them, though their interests in the land were very different. France was looking to establish settlements as England had along the coast. Spain feared that France was interested in attacking Mexico City and taking the gold that the Spanish conquistadors had found. The northern region was a buffer that kept them safe. By the time the fight between the two nations was over, most of North America had been divided between them. However, the warring countries failed to account for the growing power of Great Britain.

Spain's Initial Journey from the Gulf of Mexico to the Pacific Ocean

Spanish explorers first glimpsed the lands that are part of today's Texas back in 1519 when Alonso Álvarez de Pineda mapped the coast. Pineda was the first European to explore the Gulf of Mexico. Nearly a decade later, in 1528, Pánfilo de Narváez and Álvar Núñez Cabeza de Vaca left Spain to do a more intense exploration of the lands beyond the coast. Many of the initial explorers on this trip died. Cabeza de Vaca reached land with less than ninety men on his vessel, and they were shipwrecked near what today is called Galveston Island. His ship included Estevanico, an African who had been enslaved. Estevanico is thought to have been the first person of direct African descent to have reached North America. The Karankawa tribe in the area took pity on the shipwrecked Spaniards, giving them food and shelter. Despite the aid of the native peoples, only fifteen of de Vaca's eighty men survived the winter.

Cabeza de Vaca and his remaining men would continue their quest to learn more about the land, spending eight years moving across the vast area in the southern region of North America. They did not take a straight path but followed a somewhat circuitous route, first going south before heading almost directly north. He and his small group made their way across the land largely unhampered by the native peoples, who did not see such a small party as a threat. Working as both a healer and a trader, de Vaca traveled across Texas, trying to reach Mexico City. During his initial trip south, de Vaca and his men encountered three other members of the original expedition who had been separated from them by the shipwreck. The three men had been enslaved by one of the native tribes, believed to have been the Mariames. Cabeza de Vaca was also taken prisoner, and he would remain a prisoner for several years.

Cabeza de Vaca and his three men would finally escape the Mariames roughly six years since their expedition had begun, though exact dates are not certain. The men escaped individually but met up after their escape. The Spaniards encountered the Avavares tribe as they were trying to get out of the region, and the Avavares took them in and helped them recover. It took the four men eight months to regain their health from their time in enslavement and escape.

Once able to travel, de Vaca and his men traversed west until they were close to the Pacific Ocean. As they reached the coast, they headed south. Mexico City was already well-established, and he knew that if he could make it there, he and his men would be able to safely return to Spain. It took them about two years after their escape to reach their destination. After making it to Mexico City, the Spanish explorers quickly spread the word of more riches further north.

The rumors of more wealth made the Spanish believe that they could profit by plundering North America as they had Central and South America. It would take them about seventy years to realize that de Vaca and his men had been very much mistaken about what kind of riches could be found to the north.

A Misguided Hunt for Gold

As we know today, there is gold in North America but not nearly in the quantities that were present in Central and South America. Based on the rumors spread by de Vaca and his men, Spain would perpetually send explorers north to hunt for these riches. Initially, they believed the rumors because of the success of Francisco Vásquez de Coronado in modern-day New Mexico.

Based on those rumors, Coronado marched north with over 1,000 men in 1540. It took them about two and a half months before they reached something promising in the form of the Hawikuh Zuni pueblo. The streets were not lined with gold as Coronado's expedition expected, but he decided to claim the city of sandstone and adobe for Spain anyway. After reading the *Requerimiento* to the Zunis, he expected them to submit to Spanish rule and convert to Christianity. Naturally, the Zunis reacted by firing arrows at the invaders. The barbaric Spaniards entered the city and slaughtered most of the 500 people who lived there.

Feeling emboldened by the brutal and unjustified massacre, Coronado felt certain that they would find success if they kept marching and slaughtering all the native peoples who stood between them and riches. They turned east toward the Quivira Kingdom, believing that wealth was not far from their grasp. Of course, after crossing the Texas Panhandle, Coronado found absolutely nothing like he was expecting.

Though he successfully taught native peoples the dangers of Europeans, Coronado's expedition had been an utter failure in all other ways. When he returned home with less than he had when he left Mexico City, others became less inclined to journey north, as it was clear that they would not easily find the gold they wanted.

Ironically, as Coronado was heading back to Mexico City emptyhanded, Luis de Moscoso de Alvarado accidentally stumbled into modern-day Texas from the eastern side. Hernando de Soto and his men, including Alvarado, had explored Florida searching for the same gold that they simply would never find in the region. De Soto died from an illness during the spring of 1542, which left Alvarado less inclined to continue the hunt for riches, and he marched instead to Mexico City. They raided and plundered the Caddo people as they trekked west, teaching native people on the other end of the state the brutality and uncivilized methods used by Europeans to get what they wanted. Seeking to rid themselves of the vicious Spanish, one of the Caddo chiefs had his men guide Alvarado to a region with far fewer resources. When Alvarado realized what had been done, he had the guides killed. The Spanish headed down the Mississippi River to the Gulf of Mexico, reaching Mexico in the fall of 1542. His arrival confirmed what Coronado had already discovered earlier in the year: there were no riches to the north.

After dual warnings of no wealth, the only reason the Spanish went north over the next seventy years was to recover men who had gone missing. These explorers accepted assistance from the natives who were willing to help them, particularly the Jumano. Antonio de Espejo led one such expedition to find missing men, and he took a much more scholarly approach to the endeavor. He documented the trip, detailing the many different landscapes and tribes that they encountered. The Jumano provided many of the details for his journal. However, based on Espejo's findings, the Spanish in Mexico had no desire to explore further because they were only interested in wealth.

It wasn't until 1598 that the Spanish would again decide to do something in the northern regions. Juan de Oñate was tasked with establishing a settlement in what is currently New Mexico. He still harbored hope that he would get rich and was disappointed when he also discovered that there was no gold or silver paving any of the lands he visited. He claimed the modern-day El Paso region for Spain, but he didn't stay and settle as he had been ordered to do. What Oñate did find was a trade route that was well-established by the native peoples, and Spain would begin to use it to get the supplies that they did not have in Mexico City. Apart from trade, Spain did very little with the northern regions they had claimed. At the time, they believed that the lands were theirs and that there was no reason to further press their claim because no other European nations appeared interested in them.

France Seeks to Settle along the Mississippi River

France had been exploring North America during the 17th century, looking for something much different than what the Spanish desired. Like the British, the French were hoping to get rich from what they could produce in the region, not by what they could plunder from cities. In 1685, France finally made a move that the Spanish took note of: they tried to settle along the Mississippi River. At the time, the Spanish had laid claim to much of the territory between Florida and

Texas, so they saw this as a move against them, particularly as it would divide Spanish contact with Florida.

René Robert Cavalier, Sieur de la Salle left France in 1684 to set up a new settlement. England had settlements in the "new world," so France wanted to claim some of the fertile regions in the south. The explorer and his crew managed to miss the Mississippi River, landing in a region that today is part of Texas, a region that the Spanish definitely believed they owned by 1685. Spain knew that the French were coming and were upset when the French settlers landed on their turf. Starting in 1686, the Spanish sent explorers into Texas and would continue to send a total of nine expeditions until 1691 to find where the French had settled. They only found a few surviving settlers, and many of the French went back to Mexico City after giving up on the settlement.

France wouldn't try to settle the region again until 1699. This time, the settlements were successful, and France managed to settle several areas between the eastern coast of Tejas and what is now modern-day New Orleans. By this point, Spain had already given up trying to settle the regions because of a series of misfortunes, including flooding and Native American aggression against them.

Chapter 3 – Spanish Settlers Claim the Region

Spanish missionaries and other religious figures had moved into the northern regions of the Americas, including parts of Texas, and managed to establish friendly relationships with the natives, including the Caddo people who had given the region its name. For a few hundred years, they and soldiers would be the only Spanish citizens who would brave the region. However, the relationship quickly soured as the Spanish gave the native peoples many reasons to distrust them, including forced labor, cheating on trade agreements, and other actions that the conquistadors became notorious for committing against native peoples in the Americas. The native peoples had also noticed by this point how unhygienic the Europeans were and how many plagues and diseases seemed to follow them, killing the indigenous who had no immunities to European illnesses. Nor was the relationship between the monks and the soldiers particularly good. They each had their own set of rules: one group followed the rules of the Spanish government and the other followed the rules of the church.

Tribes like the Apache would eventually leave, but the Spanish had established a foothold in several different parts of Texas. As France and England had growing settlements on the continent, these Texan regions became more important to Spain because they provided protection for the larger Spanish settlements in the Central and South

American regions. After successfully removing the French from the region, Spain wanted to ensure that they did not lose any land to other empires. The Spanish then founded San Antonio in 1718 to dissuade other European nations from moving further west.

The First Governor and Eastern Settlements

While most of the Spanish explorers didn't have much interest in the region north of Mexico City, Spanish members of the Roman Catholic Church saw potential. By the early 1700s, the Spanish Crown had realized the threat posed by the French, and, to deter them from trying to settle in lands that the Spanish had claimed, the Spanish Crown decided to designate a governor of the region. The first person to be appointed to the post was General Domingo Terán de los Rios. He was charged with managing Coahuila, Texas, and the surrounding area. He focused on establishing settlements to the east near the area where the French had tried to build their first settlement. Monks of the Franciscan order first moved east with the Spanish soldiers to help establish these settlements. The soldiers were meant to protect the settlement and guard the land, while the Franciscan priests would build missions and convert the local populations to the east. New missions were formed near the Rio Grande and then into western Texas as the settlements proved to be beneficial, if not enriching, to Spain.

The settlements were called presidios (fortifications), and they were fortified to ensure that the settlers were safe. These were primarily where the soldiers and other settlers lived, and the walls provided a place for secular needs, such as enforcing laws and housing soldiers. The Franciscans had their own establishments in the missions they built. Both missions and presidios were built in the same area, and they worked together (similar to how churches, courthouses, and other government buildings were often the central buildings in new towns in American settlements about 100 years later).

The Franciscans were not required to follow the laws of the soldiers and other civilians. They had their own laws based on the Roman Catholic Church, which were above the laws of the non-clergy. This resulted in tensions between the missions and the presidios, mostly because the Franciscans often decried the abuses their countrymen perpetrated against the native peoples. The abuses of the secular Spanish went against the teachings of the priests, and it made their attempts to convert natives considerably more difficult. The secular settlers resented the fact that the Franciscans did not have to follow their laws. They were equally upset with the frequency with which the Franciscans would oppose their attempts to rule over the native peoples. Technically, the newly converted people were part of the missions, not the presidios. This went against everything that the Spanish had been doing since their arrival in the New World, and they believed that the religious men were undermining their efforts to control the population.

The Spanish monarchy did not intercede in these squabbles because it did not have the same goals or interests as the settlers. To the Spanish government, the settlements were simply a buffer against any encroachment on their lands that could result in loss of the gold they were still seeking in the lands further south.

The First Settlements

The Franciscans largely decided where settlements would be built because they were primarily interested in occupying the lands. They saw the native people as potential converts, which was a much greater form of wealth to them than gold. The first successful settlements during the 1680s were in San Angelo, El Paso, and Presidio, all in the area that is currently New Mexico. As they then began to work to create the buffer zone in the eastern portion of the region, the first real Texas towns were established. The very first was in what is now San Antonio. They also established a settlement in an area that had been abandoned by the Caddo, a place called Nacogdoches. Missions began to try to integrate with the native populations, most notably the Apache. However, none of these missions lasted for long, and the native peoples usually were not sincere in their conversion. Their interest lay more in how the Spanish could protect them from aggressive tribes than in forgoing their deities and religions.

While many of the settlements did not last, the buildings that were made during this time were incredibly durable. Among the most famous buildings made during the period of Spanish missionary settlements was the Alamo. However, these settlements were not made to be protective; they were made to be convenient places for gatherings and for the missionaries to work with the native peoples. These settlements were largely open and inviting, though some military fortifications were added since soldiers were present as well. The fortifications were made to protect the Spanish and their native allies against other hostile native tribes. Considering these tribes used less advanced weapons, the settlements did not need the kind of robust protection as the regions near other European settlers.

Rising Concerns Following the Louisiana Purchase

Spain and its colonies thought they had a decent buffer established against the French. After all, the French did not have many settlements in the region, and it was easy to ensure that they did not encroach on the Spanish lands. In 1803, Spain became very concerned with the future of its territory in North America when the French sold a large percentage of the lands claimed by France to the young United States. Suddenly, there was a much larger, more immediate threat to the Spanish territory. Americans were not only much closer but also more numerous on the continent. It was only a matter of time before American settlers moved west to explore their new acquisition from the French. There was no guarantee that the settlers would know which lands were theirs and which belonged to Spain.

Perhaps of greater concern was the fact that the region of Texas had never been well-defined. Initially, Spain and the US tried to avoid problems by establishing a fifty-mile wide neutral area. Despite this effort to keep the peace, tensions were not eased. Spain had reason to be concerned because of the American's growing belief in Manifest Destiny. After the young nation had acquired such an expansive region, it began to believe its God-given destiny was to rule over all the land between the Atlantic and Pacific Oceans. This was not a well-formed idea initially because the Americans did not have any knowledge of those lands. However, more the Americans explored and learned more, there was a growing, though unfounded, belief that they were destined to incorporate most of North American into their nation. This meant obtaining the lands controlled by Spain.

Ironically, Spain would try to solve its problem by inviting Americans to settle in their territory. The Americans would end up being less of a problem for Spain than it had anticipated, as it was the Spanish settlers who would ultimately rebel against them. Just seven years after the Louisiana Purchase, the War for Mexican Independence began. Spain lost interest in the actions of the American settlers in Texas because they stood to lose a lot more as their people in Mexico rebelled. Texas had always been viewed as simply a buffer area to protect the lands that were now demanding independence from Spain. Spain's primary concern from 1810 on would be retaining its colonies rather than stemming the flood of American settlers, whom it would invite into the region in just a few years as the Mexican War for Independence dragged on.

Chapter 4 – Americans Settle

Realizing that they couldn't possibly colonize all their new land, the Spanish decided the best way to make the most of those lands was to invite the Americans to come and settle. Americans had been profiting off the land across North America for a few centuries by this point, something the Spanish hadn't genuinely attempted to do. Starting in 1820, Spain invited their northern neighbors to settle, with a few stipulations. This invitation was extended despite the political upheaval in the area—Spain's hold over Mexico was precarious, at best.

When the War for Mexican Independence ended, the new Mexican government had to decide whether to honor the invitation that Spain had extended. Any Americans who had made an agreement with Spain would now also need to make a similar agreement with the new Mexican government before they would be able to settle. This was complicated by the arrival of Americans in Texas prior to the war's end. Ultimately, Mexico would allow the settlers to stay and continue to allow new settlers into the region if they met similar conditions to those that were set by Spain.

Successful Settlements Prior to the American Settlements

Despite numerous attempts by the Spanish missionaries and soldiers to create viable areas to live, by 1820, there were only three established Texas settlements: La Bahía del Espíritu Santo (which would later become Goliad), Nacogdoches, and San Antonio de Bexar. These settlements were small towns that had a few ranches dotting the area around them.

One of the primary reasons that so many of their other attempts failed was the increasing hostility of Comanche and Kiowa, who did not like the Spaniards invading their territory. Unlike the Caddo and Apache, the Comanche and Kiowa saw no benefit in allowing the Spanish to have footholds in lands that their tribes had occupied for generations, especially because the Spanish had made it clear that they considered themselves superior. Despite this Spanish belief of superiority, the Native Americans were easily able to destroy or to accelerate the failure of several settlements.

The religious laws that had ruled when the three successful settlements were established were largely abandoned by this time, and the mission in Nacogdoches had been closed before the end of the 18th century. As the settlements became more secular, there was increasingly more reason to allow others to take on the incredibly difficult task of creating settlements on Native land. Spain was more accustomed to taking over settled areas, not in creating safe havens in open terrain. Americans had already proven to be very adept at turning "untamed" lands into profitable towns. Spain hoped to profit from this ingenuity without having to do much more than offer Americans land.

Conditions for Settling in Texas

Though the Spanish had positioned themselves to bar European countries from their lands, they took a different approach with their northern neighbors. During the last years of the 18th century, Spain had invited Americans to settle in their lands near Upper Louisiana. Using the offer they had made during that time as a template, Spain tried to lure Americans further west. In exchange for land in Texas, Americans would need to

agree to three requirements.

Spain had long been a proponent of the Roman Catholic Church, while most of the US was Protestant. These were considered incompatible, so one of the most important stipulations the Spanish made was that any Americans settling in their lands convert to Roman Catholicism. Almost as important was the second stipulation that the American settlers would be loyal to Spain, not the US. This meant that they would need to renounce their American citizenship and become Spanish citizens. However, American settlers would not have the same rights as people who were born Spanish citizens. This inequality was not obvious, and if the settlers realized it, they likely decided that it wouldn't matter much since they would be living far away from the large Spanish settlements. To protect their investment, Spain also insisted that the American settlers primarily trade with them instead of the US. It was a calculated risk that the Spanish hoped would boost their economy, especially during the war for Mexican Independence.

Empresarios (as potential settlers were called) could request a grant from Spain, and if approved, they would be able to establish their settlements. The empresarios would be responsible for the people who settled under their agreement, a stipulation that Mexico would also adopt when they later made agreements with the empresarios.

Americans were more than happy to agree to the conditions in exchange for inexpensive land. The cost of land in the US was $1.25 per acre, and they were required to buy at least eighty acres for a total of $100. Spain was offering the head of a family (whether a man or a woman) 4,605 acres for only $184, which could be paid over a six-year period instead of all at once. This attracted the attention of scores of Americans who sought to make their own fortunes.

Another reason so many Americans were willing to move was that they expected the US to eventually purchase the region from Spain. By this time, Manifest Destiny was a belief shared by many Americans, though neither Spain nor Mexico would understand that this belief also applied to them and not just to the native peoples. Had the Spanish realized that Americans expected to take over the whole region, they likely would have taken the same protective stance against Americans as they had against the French, instead of openly inviting Americans onto the northern lands of Mexico.

Finally, there were Americans who were fleeing from the law and deportation, the most notable of which was the Austin family. Though Stephen Austin's father, Moses Austin, had brokered a deal with Spain to settle 300 people in Texas, he died before the settlers reached their destination. It was left to Stephen to make a new agreement with Mexico for the settlers. He renegotiated for the group, but nothing was mentioned about criminals and debtors. Without an agreement between the US and Mexico to extradite criminals, Texas could be a haven for many people who were in financial trouble and had opted to move west to avoid debt collectors and the law.

A Change in Government

Mexico won its independence in 1821. Among the many things they needed to establish was how to deal with the Americans who had made agreements with Spain to settle Texas. While those agreements were now void because Spain no longer had any power in the region, several empresarios (the most well-known of which was Stephen Austin) were planning to move hundreds of Americans into the region.

Mexico agreed to renegotiate the terms of the agreements, largely keeping things the same. One notable difference was that settlers need only profess that they were Christian, not specifically Roman Catholic. The predominant religion in Mexico was Catholic, and it was likely implied that the settlers should become Catholic. However, they avoided specifying that the settlers would need to convert. They further made it clear that the settlers' religion was not a primary concern: they did not even provide a priest for any of the settlements until 1831. This meant that many of the Americans could not complete basic religious ceremonies. Most notably, they could not marry without a priest present. Many resorted to establishing marriage bonds and then making them official when the priest finally arrived.

Though Austin was the first empresario, Mexico would go on to make individual agreements with about thirty empresarios, resulting in the arrival of about 9,000 families. Initially, Austin only had 300 settlers. Each empresario had their own agreement with a set number of people they could bring to the region. This was how Mexico attempted to control the number of Americans that settled on their lands. All the contracts clearly defined where the settlers were permitted to establish their new homes and how much land each family could have. The empresarios always got more than the people who came along with them, but, with so much land available, settlers usually accepted the disparity in land distribution. All contracts were six years long, during which time settlers would have to pay for their land. Payments were usually based on what they had earned from the land. The last contractual settlement was with the Mercer colony, signed in January 1844.

A Question of How to Handle Slaves

Slavery had been one of the primary reasons that the farmers and plantations in the US had been successful. Spain and Mexico both knew that the Americans would not come without slaves to prop up their settlements. Though both Spain and Mexico did not want slavery in their lands, they were willing to allow the first settlers to bring slaves so that the Americans could be financially successful. Mexico hoped to benefit financially, in turn.

Slaves were not allowed to be sold in Texas, but initially, settlers were permitted to bring slaves they already owned. Once in Texas, settlers could buy and sell or trade slaves among themselves, though new slaves were not permitted to be brought in specifically for selling. This agreement stood until 1840. However, some officials signaled their unwillingness to allow slavery to continue for much longer in the settlements. It was hinted as early as 1827 that the practice of slavery would be ended and slaves emancipated at some point. In response, slave owners set up indentured servant contracts with their illiterate slaves that tied the slaves to them for ninety-nine years, essentially keeping Mexico from being able to emancipate them.

Mexican officials were not pleased with this move, but they did not do anything to stop it. The most forceful step to stop slavery in Texas came from President Vicente Ramón Guerrero, who declared emancipation in September 1829. Several of the empresarios quickly deployed to Mexico City to try to get an exemption from the emancipation.

The question of slavery would be as much a point of contention between American settlers and Mexico as it was between the northern and southern states in the US.

Stephen Austin and the Formation of the Texas Rangers

As the first empresario, Austin had much more autonomy and control than subsequent empresarios. His negotiations with Mexico would often be implemented across other settlements. With little to no support from Mexico, Austin was responsible for those who wanted to immigrate into the land Mexico had allowed him to settle. The Mexican government did not want too many foreigners populating their lands, but they also did not have the capability to provide any legal assistance or protection to the incoming people. The burden of creating and enforcing law and order and distributing land, as well as creating all the settlement's social infrastructure—such as roads, schools, granaries, and sawmills—fell on Austin.

Perhaps the most difficult job Austin had was dealing with the Mexican government, though. Mexico was not able to help the settlers but still expected the settlers to follow Mexican laws. This included a ban on slaves, which the American settlers refused to relinquish. Despite the desire to keep all people marginally free in Mexico, Austin negotiated for the Americans' ability to keep their slaves after the Mexican government banned the institution in 1829.

With criminals coming to the area to escape the laws in the US and Native Americans fighting to keep the settlers off their lands, Austin decided that he needed to form a group that could both protect the settlers and provide law enforcement. While Austin was in Mexico City working to safeguard the rights to continued settlement, one of his lieutenants, Moses Morrison, formed a militia to protect the settlers. The militia consisted of ten men who swore to rise to the occasion when needed. Morrison assembled this small contingent to go to the Texas coast, where the Karankawa and Tonkawa tribes were continually attacking the settlers.

When Austin returned from Mexico, he doubled the number of men to twenty, all of them paid volunteers. Each volunteer was offered fifteen dollars a month, though the payment was often in land instead of money. In the early days, the men were called for a variety of different needs, and the militia was not permanent. When their services were not needed, the volunteers would be disbanded so that they could care for their families. The first volunteers consisted of a very diverse range of individuals, including Hispanics, Anglos, and Native Americans. The combined talents of these individuals made a highly effective volunteer militia. These twenty men would be the first members of the organization that would come to be known as the Texas Rangers.

Chapter 5 – Rising Tensions between Mexico and the Settlements

Resentment between American settlers and the Mexican government grew quickly after the settlements were established. The settlers had been dissatisfied with the agreements that they had made with Mexico, particularly the stipulation that they would eventually have to give up their slaves. Mexico began to resent how many of the American settlers were completely disregarding the agreements that they had made. The empresarios were not controlling the flow of immigrants into the region, and consequently, Mexico was losing its grip on large swaths of Texas land.

The expectation that the Americans would be grateful for the land and would agree to live by Mexican laws proved to be a serious miscalculation. The more control Mexico tried to exert over their territories, the more resentful the Americans became. After all, the Americans had established their own way of life largely without Mexican assistance. The Texas Rangers had been formed to protect American settlers because the Mexican government could not spare the men to protect them, and Americans in the region had become accustomed to enforcing their own laws. The idea that Mexico expected them to abide by their agreements seemed incomprehensible to the Americans, who disregarded the few requirements they were given in exchange for a new life and a lot of land.

The Effects of the Mexican War of Independence

Having won their independence from Spain, Mexico had hoped that the settlers would be able to turn the lands into something profitable. Like the Spanish before them, the Mexicans did not want to extend the same rights to the settlers that their native-born enjoyed. Americans were considered inferior to the people in power, who were largely wealthy former Spaniards. With both sides viewing each other as inferior people, it was only a matter of time before these views caused more serious problems.

Mexico had won its independence at a very high cost both in terms of lives and resources, and the new country was facing serious financial devastation when the war ended in 1821. The mines that had once produced a considerable amount of money under Spanish control were not nearly as efficient under the new government. Food production was also significantly reduced as Mexicans sought to earn more money through other endeavors. Unemployment was another significant problem; there was not enough money in circulation to pay workers, which further drove people to emigrate in the hopes of finding work and a livelihood. Unrest and other serious problems were further exacerbated by the large class disparity within the fledgling country.

The settlements had become accustomed to the laisse faire approach that the Mexican people took toward the settlements. Of course, Mexico couldn't provide much support, but it also meant that they didn't interfere in the way settlements were run. The empresarios were pretty much their governmental leaders, or at least that was largely how they saw it. However, once the Mexican government was formed, it expected that the settlers would begin to heed its demands. This diverse view of the role of the Mexican government in the settlers' lives was further complicated by the kind of people who became the leaders of the new Mexican government. Those who rose to leadership within the Mexican government had very little experience in governing; they were not prepared to deal with the rising problems. This led to the wealthy, religious figures, and military leaders stepping into more prominent roles to retain the class structure that had existed under Spanish rule. While they had wanted freedom from Spain, most of the people in these three social groups did not want equality. By ensuring that the antebellum order continued in the new country, the gentry, church officials, and military leaders would have equal control over the direction of the government—much more than they would have enjoyed had Spain continued to control the region. To all the powerful parties in Mexico, the American settlers seemed to be a perfect solution to some of their problems: they would help improve the financial situation in Mexico while protecting the country from further US expansion.

Settlers had long been dealing with a problem that the former Spanish citizens had not—they had survived amid the constant attacks of the native peoples in the north. The lands were populated with Native Americans who were not welcoming of invaders, and they did not recognize Mexico as owners of their ancestral homelands (just as they had not acknowledged the theft of these lands by Spain). Mexico had too many problems to contend with to quell the threat that the native peoples posed. By leaving the settlers to contend with the Native Americans, Mexico wouldn't have to worry about being attacked by those groups. They had enough problems in Mexico City as different factions tried to take control of the government to contend with the issues posed by the northern regions. Essentially, Mexico hoped the settlers would distract the native population, making the native peoples an American problem. Even as the settlers slaughtered the natives that Mexico could not fight, the Mexicans somehow thought that they would be better able to control the Americans than they had the natives. This would quickly prove to be untrue.

In 1824, Mexico passed a national colonization law, intended to supersede the older imperial colonization law, and it changed the way the Mexican territory would be populated and governed. Instead of dealing with the Mexican government directly, people wishing to establish new contracts to settle in the territory would need to go to the state legislatures. Many of the states hoped they could have greater control over themselves and attempted to mimic how the US states largely self-governed, with minimal interference from the federal government. While the 1824 Federal Constitution of the United Mexican States took much of its inspiration from the Constitution of the United States of America, it also included some of the tenets that had been written in the Spanish Constitution of 1812. This change would prove to be significant, as the states were better able to monitor the settlers than the Mexican federal government had. They also took a greater interest in who was settling their lands.

Two of the main states located in the northern region were Texas and Coahuila. Ultimately, both would become a part the American state called Texas, but during the 18th century, they were separate. Under the jurisdiction of Nuevo Santander, both territories had their own missions, but in 1716, they were governed by Martin de Alarcon.

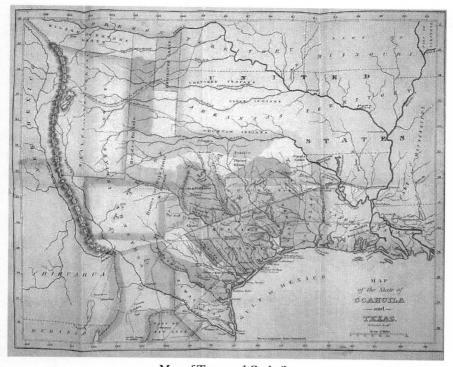

Map of Texas and Coahuila
*https://commons.wikimedia.org/wiki/File:Hooker_Map_of_the_State_of_Coahuila_and_Tex
as_1834_UTA.jpg*

Implementing the New Mexican Laws

Following the passing of the new law, government leaders met in Saltillo, the capital of the Mexican state of Coahuila, to establish the rules for determining who could settle the northern lands and what requirements must be followed. The officials in Saltillo would set the requirements and define the terms of any agreement with empresarios in Texas, which meant that they would also determine who would receive the contracts, whether the applicants were American, European, or Mexican. These rules were documented in the state colonization law.

The focus of the government leaders was largely on ranching and farming to produce more food and encourage the growth of commerce in the region among the different settlements. According to the new law, Mexicans would have the first choice of land in settling the northern region; then, Americans would be allowed to settle. Although they would be required to pay for the land where they settled, initially immigrants would not be taxed as they strove to establish themselves. All they needed to do was agree to be bound by the contract their empresario had signed and take an oath that they would abide by its requirements, including becoming Mexican citizens. Once the oath was completed, settlers became naturalized Mexicans.

Problems arose when the federal government realized how much the settlers were neglecting the oath they had taken. Many of the Americans were failing to live up to the few requirements of the oath, retaining their own traditions instead of integrating with the Mexican traditions and people. More egregiously, Americans did not adopt Mexican laws in their settlements. They blatantly disregarded the laws that were inconvenient to their way of life and implemented their own local laws instead, some of which contradicted Mexican laws.

Growing Resentment

Nearly a decade before Texas instigated a war for independence, other American settlers were already expressing a desire to revolt against the Mexican government. The first such revolt was precipitated by a man named Haden Edwards. Edwards and the settlers in his colony declared independence in 1826, calling their land the Republic of Fredonia. They had planned to work with the Cherokee to form an alliance and create a new flag representing the Americans and native peoples. After signing a declaration of independence in December of 1826, they turned to the US for support. They also asked Stephen Austin to assist them in their fight against the Mexican government. Predictably, Austin sided with the Mexican government, and he joined the Mexicans in putting down the rebellion. By the end of January 1827, the Republic of Fredonia was no more. Unhappy that they had been dragged into such a poorly-planned rebellion, the Cherokee killed the main leaders, John Dunn Hunter and Richard Fields. Haden Edwards survived by fleeing and would later return to join in the War of Texas Independence.

Mexico was understandably shaken by this apparently unprovoked call for independence and became wary of allowing any further American settlers into its territories. Since it had been the responsibility of the federal government, not the state government, to put down the rebellion, leaders of the Mexican government began to try to consolidate power. Desiring to build a much stronger central government that more closely copied the way that Spain had ruled, they began drafting new laws toward the end of 1829 and passed them in April of 1830. The new laws voided any existing agreement with the settlers if the settlers were not complying with the terms of that agreement, in addition to curtailing American immigration. The only exceptions to this were the settlements under Stephen Austin and Green DeWitt. The Mexican government found that these two empresarios had fulfilled their requirements (something that was not completely true for either of the two men). The Mexican government also established military outposts so they could prevent new American settlers from entering Mexico and Texas. No more slaves would be allowed to be brought into the country, though slaves who currently resided there would remain enslaved.

For the five years prior to the new agreement, both Coahuila and the American settlers had greatly benefited from the relationship they had established. In fact, they were prospering in a way that had eluded much of the rest of Mexico. Commerce had become stable and was even lucrative in some regions. The federal government's interference threatened both the free commerce that had been established as well as the sovereignty of Coahuila. Slaves had been allowed to be brought into Coahuila because there were not enough people to work the lands without them. However, they were now to be indentured, giving them the ability to earn money to buy their own freedom. Under the new laws, though, it would no longer be possible to bring in new slaves, and people in the Texan territory feared that this would reduce their ability to conduct commerce and simultaneously stunt growth. It was suspected that eliminating the ability to bring any more slaves into Mexico was meant to deter the kinds of Americans who often came. The Mexicans believed that if Americans could not bring their slaves, they would not be tempted to enter the country without authorization. The rise in anti-immigration laws resulted in much greater hostility between the Anglo-Americans and Mexicans and did not have the desired effect of cooling the situation. The settlers perceived this as the Mexicans interfering in the territories that were under settler control, proving that they still saw themselves as Americans, not as Mexicans. Both the resistance to follow Mexican laws and immigration requirements understandably upset the Mexican leaders.

A Mexican politician and general named Santa Anna acted in 1833 to alleviate the issue. He led the government in revoking the law that had institutionalized immigration discrimination, and the effects were nearly immediate, as Americans began to immigrate into the regions that had been prospering under the better-established settlements. Roughly a year later, Santa Anna would reverse his decision to allow greater states' rights. He called for the congregation of a new congress that would create a strong central government. It took nearly a year, but the country was reconfigured in the fall of 1835, with states being converted into departments that would then be controlled by presidential appointees.

This did not sit well with the people in Coahuila, particularly the people in Stephen Austin's settlement. Mexico was embroiled in a civil war by this time, which made it the opportune time for Texans to finally break from the nation that had invited them to settle the lands that belonged to the Native Americans.

Chapter 6 – The Fight for Texas Independence Begins

Within ten years of Mexico finally gaining its independence from Spain, Americans decided that they needed to fight to become independent from what they saw as the dictatorial control of the Mexican government. Some of the primary American empresarios, such as Stephen Austin, sought to find a peaceful resolution and ended up caught in a fight between their settlers and the Mexican government. Though it was already facing a civil war, Mexico soon found itself fighting another internal battle—this time with the very people it had hoped would help the country prosper. Almost from the beginning, the Americans made it obvious that they had no desire to integrate into their host nation's culture or respect the oaths they took when they settled in Mexican territory. As the Mexican people were preoccupied with civil war, the Americans saw their opportunity to do what they had largely expected (or in some cases intended) to happen: they sought to remove themselves from Mexican oversight and find a way to be annexed to the US.

The Final Straw

After Mexico appointed a representative to govern the regions, the American settlers— particularly those living in Coahuila—let their anger at the move be known. Up to this point, they had largely been left to their own devices. Government oversight of the nation where they lived was considered dictatorial. Ironically, the American settlers turned to another federal government that was much more hands-on, proving that their problem was more with the fact that they were supposed to become Mexican rather than remain American.

While US states did have a considerable amount of autonomy, the US federal government had much input on how things were run within the states. In fact, the struggle between states' rights and the federal role was a problem that was proving to be very much at the forefront of US consciousness at the time. But the rebellion of the American settlers in Mexico was more about the fear of losing their way of life than in any actual problem. The threat of losing their slaves was a primary concern, and the right to own slaves was something they knew that the US would preserve if they could get the US to annex their region.

Fearing the rise of the settlers against the government, particularly as the settlers became more vocal, the Mexican commander in Coahuila requested reinforcements to quell the unrest of the settlers. As word spread that a military force was being raised against them, William B. Travis led a group of Texans to attack Anahuac in June of 1835. When they refused to surrender, Mexico took this as a direct rebellion against Mexican laws. With this direct violation of the oath the settlers had taken, war was all but inevitable.

Perhaps one of the worst things that Mexico did to disenfranchise the settled Americans was to try to make an example of the person who was most loyal to Mexico. Austin had constantly insisted that the people who settled as a part of his agreement always abide by Mexican law. In return, Austin's settlement thrived and had significantly better protection than that of any other settlement, as well as large portions of Mexico. When the Mexican government decided to make an example of Austin by imprisoning him after he tried to negotiate a peaceful resolution, Mexico managed to turn its best ally against itself. After a year of imprisonment, even Stephen Austin called for an independent Texas. When Austin returned to his settlement in 1835, Texas made their move to break away from Mexico.

Open Conflict

With Austin's return after an imprisonment based on no charges, the people of Texas finally had a figurehead to lead them into a fight for independence.

The first real conflict in the fight for Texan independence was at the Battle of Gonzales in October of 1835. The fight began as a simple request that the colonists at Gonzales return a cannon that had been given to them in 1831 to help during Native American attacks. When they refused, Texas Commander Domingo de Ugartechea sent 100 soldiers to retrieve the cannon. Knowing that the tension would make the situation precarious, de Ugartechea instructed the leader, Lieutenant Francisco de Castañeda, to avoid conflict if possible, but did say that force was acceptable if necessary. On September 27, 1835, the Mexicans left San Antonio for Gonzales. After two days, they arrived at their destination only to find that they could not cross the Guadalupe River because of flooding and the presence of eighteen American militiamen. Castañeda told the eighteen men that he had a dispatch for Andrew Ponton, and he was told that the alcalde (the Spanish name for a mayor or magistrate) was not present. While Castañeda's men pitched their camp on the opposite side of the river, the people in Gonzales requested reinforcements.

A member of the Coushatta tribe made his way into the Mexican camp and informed Castañeda that the number of men in Gonzales ready to fight was 140 or more. Instead of staying put out in the open, Castañeda had the camp broken down and forded the river further away. The soldiers set up a new camp on October 1, about seven miles from their destination.

The men in Gonzales did not sit still as they saw the Mexicans leave. Crossing the river to where the Mexicans had originally made camp, they worked their way along the river until they found the new camp. On October 2, they attacked the Mexican camp. When the first round of fighting ceased, Castañeda requested a parley. The commander of the rebels was John Henry Moore, and he agreed to the parley. While he learned that Castañeda agreed with much of the ideas that the settlers had, Castaneda could not go against his orders to retrieve the cannon. When it became clear that the fighting would resume, Castaneda knew that his side could not win. Though he and his men had been attacked without provocation, he wanted to minimize the fighting. Calling for a retreat, the Mexicans returned to Commander Ugartechea.

The battle was little more than a short skirmish over the presence of a cannon, but the victory was the sign the settlers needed to help them decide it was the time to finally engage in open war. Austin was called to be the commander of the forces fighting for Texas separation, though he was not a military man. He was a diplomat, as would quickly become obvious. He was soon replaced by Sam Houston and assumed the role of envoy to the US. Austin spent most of the war trying to convince the US to intervene on behalf of Texas. His efforts failed because the US did not want to start a war with Mexico. The US was not as divided as Mexico, but it was already plagued with many internal struggles, with slavery one of the greatest concerns.

The Texas Declaration of Independence and How the Texas Rangers Earned a More Prominent Role in the New Country

Following the events at Gonzales, the settlers convened, and a consultation drafted the Texas Declaration of Independence on November 7, 1835. It was signed by fifty-nine men, three of whom were Mexican descendants. This showed that some people who had settled the region had a sense of entitlement. On some levels, this seems natural because, up to this point, the settlers had fended for themselves. However, the declaration was in direct opposition to what the settlers had agreed to when they moved to the region. Nothing that had happened was unexpected. The people knew that they would be on the frontier, making a living for themselves. The problem was that they had grown to believe that Manifest Destiny was all but guaranteed, particularly since Mexico had done little to demonstrate an interest in their settlements. The instability of the Mexican government was a serious problem, even for those of Mexican descent, so some decided to join the other settlers instead of siding with the country that had not provided them with much support.

By 1836, the Texas Revolution had begun, and it was going well for the Texans almost from the beginning. During this time, volunteers and soldiers played a major role in the victory for Texas Independence, but the Texas Rangers had an equally crucial role. As the soldiers were focused on fighting the Mexicans, the settlers were easy targets for both Native Americans and the Mexican military. This was the first recorded instance where the Texas Rangers received a government sanction to patrol the frontiers against the Native Americans. Some of the members of the Rangers also fought against the Mexican government, but most of the forces worked to protect the settlers while others fought in the war for Texan independence. As the Rangers were adept trackers, some of them were called on to act as scouts. Also, because they were familiar with the lands, others served as carriers.

After the disaster at the Alamo (in modern-day San Antonio) in March of 1836, the Rangers went to help the Texans fleeing from the area. They assisted in getting settlers to safety and destroyed anything left behind so that it could not be used by the Mexicans, including produce from the farms. When the Rangers were called to act as escorts at the Battle of San Jacinto in April of 1836, many of them were annoyed with their role. They preferred either to fight in the war against the Mexicans or against the Native Americans. The menial tasks assigned to them during the war seemed to be a step down from their usual duties, which had been important when the area was a part of Mexican Texas. However, their role began to undergo a significant shift following the close of the war, largely because they became the only established law enforcement group in Texas. How the Rangers were used by the new government varied depending on the governor in charge, but their place and role in the new country began to solidify.

Chapter 7 – "Remember the Alamo" and Other Major Battles

One of the most notorious events in US history occurred in a territory that didn't even belong to the United States, and it was an illegal attempt by some Americans to steal lands from another nation. Of course, that isn't quite the way many Americans have portrayed it. As the Americans in Texas began to feel that Mexicans were demonstrating authoritarian tendencies, some began to believe that they didn't need to continue to follow any of their agreements with the nation of Mexico.

While the Americans thought they were fighting for independence from a dictatorial government, Mexico believed that the Americans were in breach of their agreement and were stealing lands that belonged to Mexico. The War of Texas Independence was already being fought by the time the Americans tried to defend the old Spanish mission, but it was the events that happened there that provided a rallying cry against the Mexicans.

A Brief History of the Alamo

The Alamo was over 100 years old when its name became the rallying cry for Americans trying to establish their own country. Originally founded as a mission to convert the native peoples of the area, the structure was well constructed. It was part of the established settlements in San Antonio, making it one of the oldest European structures in the region. As the chapel for the original mission, it was erected between 1716 and 1718, though it is not known when it was finished and put to use. Over the next 100 years, Spanish soldiers would stop at the Alamo to rest during their marches across the region. The soldiers were the ones to give the structure its name, the Alamo (Spanish for cottonwood), because of the number of cottonwood trees in the region.

A Flawed Plan

As the War of Texas Independence waged on, more Americans continued to enter the territory, with many of them deciding to fight in the war. Some of them made their way west toward San Antonio, despite warnings from Sam Houston, who was the leader of the Texan military forces. The American leaders had decided it was best to leave San Antonio because it was too difficult to defend, but the volunteers disregarded their warnings. By this time, the Alamo was more than 125 years old, and it had not been well maintained. The men insisted on remaining despite being exposed to the elements and the Mexican forces.

Several famous Americans were a part of the group of volunteers who refused to give up their position. The commanders of the volunteers were James Bowie and William B. Travis. Bowie is best known for the knife that was named after him. Perhaps the best-known participant in the events at the Alamo was David (Davy) Crockett, a former congressman and frontiersman. Crockett had been disillusioned by American politics, particularly President Andrew Jackson's genocide of Native Americans. Having failed to prevent the events leading up to the Trail of Tears, Crockett left the US to make a new life in Texas. All three men had experience on the frontier, but their experience did not necessarily prepare them for an actual fight against a military force, especially not an army commanded by one of the most renowned Mexican military leaders they faced in February of 1836.

Mexican General Antonio Lopez de Santa Anna had been marching with the Mexican military west to put down the settlers' rebellion. He and an army of between 1,800 and 6,000 men (records on the number of Mexican soldiers vary) arrived at the Alamo on February 23, 1836. Upon their arrival, they began a siege of the Alamo.

A Grim Realization, an Appeal for Help, and the Birth of a Rallying Cry

When the siege began, it quickly became very clear to the American volunteers that Houston had been right in his assessment of the impossibility of protecting the region. Travis acted on this realization and sent word to anyone who could be reached, pleading with "the people of Texas & all Americans in the world" to come and support them in their ill-conceived desire to keep a structure that was neither strategic for victory nor beneficial to the larger fight.

Once in position, the Mexican military began to fire cannons on the walls of the Alamo, reducing much of the outer structure to rubble. Despite the odds, the Americans did manage to hold the Alamo for thirteen days, defending it against a much greater force. The Mexicans had an equally difficult time trying to remove the Americans because the region was not ideal for fighting.

It is said that Travis sent a woman out to act as a messenger for the Texans in the Alamo. She relayed the message that they were willing to surrender if Santa Anna would agree to spare the lives of the Texans. The response was that the people in the Alamo had to surrender with no guarantee about what would happen to them. To the Mexicans, the Texans were traitors who did not deserve any kind of concession. Once they had their answer, the people in the Alamo decided that their only option was to take out as many Mexicans as they could because there was no chance of beating such a large, well-trained force.

On March 6, 1836, the Mexicans finally decided to push forward after suffering heavy casualties; they were more exposed than the Texans hiding in the Alamo. Santa Anna ordered them to storm the Alamo through a breach in the structure's wall, and they were to spare none of the defenders. It took three attempts, but the final push forward finally broke the defenders. The Mexican soldiers followed through with Santa Anna's order to kill all the defenders, sparing the lives of only women and children. Of the 180 to 260 Americans who had been at the Alamo, it is said that only fifteen survived. The number of Mexicans who died is estimated to be between 600 and 1,600. Houston had been right about how impossible it was to fight in such an open, old area, and it had been a rather ill-advised fight for either side.

With so few survivors and the loss of some of the most notable American frontiersmen at the Alamo, many Texans were enraged. When they marched into battle about a month later, Houston led a force into battle against Santa Anna to the rallying cry of "Remember the Alamo!"

The Battle of San Jacinto and the End of the Fight for Texas Independence

The defeat at the Alamo was the first of two crushing blows; the second was the Goliad Massacre. An estimated 350 rebels were killed about a month after the disaster at the Alamo. Those who were captured during the battle were executed, giving the settlers more reason to persist. If the Texans were to give up because of the defeats, they could expect a very harsh response to the rebellion.

Santa Anna saw the two Mexican victories as a sign that the Texans would soon be defeated, leading to a serious miscalculation on his part: he divided his military to try to finish off the rebels faster. Angered by the way Santa Anna had refused to take prisoners,

General Sam Houston went after the legendary Mexican military leader. The Texan finally caught up to the smaller Mexican military at the San Jacinto River on April 21, 1836. As Santa Anna had not expected the Texans to be on the offensive, the attack took him and his men by surprise. The attack became a rout, and about half of the Mexicans were killed. Santa Anna and the rest of his men were taken prisoner. As Santa Anna was also the President of Mexico, the Texans forced him to sign an agreement that recognized Texas as an independent nation. He and his men were forced to return to Mexico.

Mexico and the Newly Independent Texas, 1838
Map of Texas and Coahuila
https://commons.wikimedia.org/wiki/File:Hooker_Map_of_the_State_of_Coahuila_and_Tex as_1834_UTA.jpg

The Republic of Texas and the Undefined Lands

With the war over, Texas and Mexico had to establish the terms for its end. The new Texas government stopped the land grant system that had dictated who controlled the lands of the new nation. Soldiers were given time to find homes as they had been the ones to sacrifice the most for the Republic of Texas.

However, there was not an agreement between Mexico and the Republic of Texas as to what the new republic included. The Republic of Texas thought that it now had more than twice the lands that had made up the few territories that made up Texas before the war. As shown below, Mexico considered the vast majority of the lands still to be in their possession. Neither of the two nations officially settled the dispute over the lands, and this would come to be a source of much larger dispute within the next two decades as the US began to finally consider what to do about the Republic of Texas, which had been looking to join the country even before they were separate from Mexico.

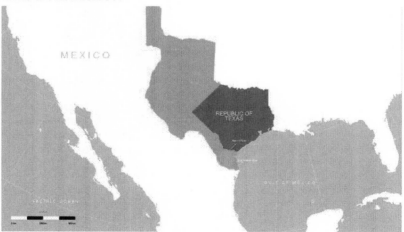

Disputed Lands between Mexico, Texas, and the US
Raymond1922A, CC BY-SA 3.0 <https://creativecommons.org/licenses/by-sa/3.0>, via Wikimedia Commons
https://commons.wikimedia.org/wiki/File:Republic_of_Texas_labeled.svg

Chapter 8 – Annexation to the US and the Mexican-American War

As Texas and Mexico fought for control of the lands that truly belonged to the native peoples, the US watched with interest. Though they were unwilling to do anything that could upset the Mexican government, they were interested in seeing how the war would be resolved. They stood to gain more from an independent Texas, and that raised the question of whether they should annex the region.

There were several very important reasons the US was hesitant to annex Texas despite Stephen Austin's pleading to intervene on behalf of the settlers, who were once American. The fear of a war with Mexico was a major concern, but there was a much more divisive problem with incorporating Texas. It involved the already strained relationship between those who wanted to abolish slavery and those who wanted to perpetuate it. However, fear of a war with Mexico was the primary reason behind US reluctance to help.

The initial refusal of the US to incorporate Texas into the country was troubling for the Texans. Having alienated nearly every group around them, the Texans knew that it was only a matter of time before their neighbors would band together to snuff them out. The Cherokee had shown a willingness to work against the Mexicans prior to the revolution, but instead of fostering this relationship, which the newly elected President Houston advocated, Texas continued to try to pressure the US into annexation.

After a decade, the US finally decided that annexing Texas was not as much of a risk as it had been during the war. It would be a messy endeavor, but by the end of the 1840s, Texas would officially become the 28th US state. After the annexation, the US instigated a war with Mexico to settle a dispute about where the boundaries of Texas should be drawn. No longer afraid of war, the US started the Mexican-American War.

Texans' Long-standing Expectations Fulfilled

The first official move to join the US came in 1836 when the first elections were held after the Texas Revolution. The people voted in favor of Texas being annexed into the US, but the Texas government failed to complete a treaty with the US that would ratify their statehood. The US was also reluctant to annex lands that had so recently been a part of Mexico.

However, once Texas had succeeded in winning its independence, the US kept an eye on the new nation and weighed its options. With more Americans streaming into Texas, some in the government also felt a sense of duty to protect those citizens. Texas did not force any of the immigrants to renounce their citizenship, so the new settlers were largely American. American settlers continued to expect protection from the US, especially as tensions with the native tribes and the Mexicans mounted. There was ample evidence that Mexico was planning to initiate an attack, with some proof manifesting during the Cherokee War.

The Joint Resolution for Annexing Texas

Though it took nearly a decade, the US government finally reached a resolution that would allow Texas to officially enter the large nation as a state. Over the years, the US government had failed to agree to an official treaty with Texas, so they switched to another tactic to bring it into the union.

There were several reasons why it took so long to annex Texas. One of the most notable concerns for the US was the debt that Texas had incurred during their war for independence. The settlers had been prosperous under the Mexican government, but they were never wealthy, and the war resulted in a large debt that the US was not willing to take on. Another major issue was the rising division in the US about slavery. Each new territory that was brought into the country had to be assessed by abolitionists and the pro-slave lobbyists to determine whether slavery would be allowed in the future state. Adding Texas would mean giving the pro-slavery contingent a large swath of land, destabilizing the delicate balance among the existing states. Texans had already shown that they had no intention of giving up their slaves, even convincing the Mexican government to allow slavery in the territory prior to the revolution.

After the Texas Revolution, Mexico had made it clear that if the US annexed Texas, Mexico would take it as a declaration of war. For this reason, the US avoided any kind of negotiation until 1844. When the US started talking to Texas about the annexation, Mexico severed all diplomatic relations. US President John Tyler was unable to get the necessary votes in the Senate to ratify a treaty that had been negotiated with Texas that year. His next bid to annex the small nation was in 1845, a few months before he was to leave office.

When the US passed a joint resolution for annexation, it included three major conditions for the would-be state. First, Texas would remain in control of its public lands and its debts; the US would not manage them, which gave Texas considerable control over its own land. The second condition partly addressed the problem of slavery by leaving an option open for the US to decide that if it wanted to divide Texas into four new states, it would have the right to do so. Finally, the US government would be responsible for providing governmental facilities, postal services, and military forces, and they would retain authority over the state as they did in all states in the union. That meant that Texas could control the land, but in exchange, they had to abide by American laws, particularly in areas where the US government was providing basic services.

By taking on Texas as a state, the US was taking a large risk. They would be building a governmental system that would run and operate on a much larger network, which would be costly. The annexation proposal was presented in July 1845 to a group of elected officials at the Constitutional Convention held in Austin. There were several proposals to consider, including the joint resolution for annexation and a peace treaty with Mexico. The peace treaty would finally settle the fighting between Texas and Mexico, but it required Texas to remain its own nation. If Texas opted to be annexed to the US, hostilities would continue. The end vote was exactly what was expected—the representatives voted to do what the people of Texas had wanted since before the Texas Revolution: to be annexed into the US. The proposal was then put to the people in October that same year. They voted to join the US, and annexation became official when the Annexation Ordinance and a state constitution were completed.

Texas submitted their votes to the US, and they were sent to Congress, where the decision of the people of Texas was quickly accepted. Before the end of 1845, the joint resolution to admit Texas into statehood was put before President James Polk for his signature. After nearly a decade of waiting, Texas was finally a state. The transfer of control began soon after, with formal transference occurring in February of 1846.

Mexico's Growing Concern

Mexican officials had been concerned that they would lose territory to the US even before the Texas war for independence. Once Texas had won its independence from Mexico without the help of the US, Mexico's fears about what could happen next intensified. Between 1836 and 1845, Mexico did everything in its power to dissuade the US from annexing the land that had so recently belonged to it.

One of the biggest points of contention between Texas and Mexico was how much of the territory belonged to Texas and how much belonged to Mexico. The total region in question would have more than doubled Texas. On its own, Texas did not pose much of a threat when it came to forcing Mexico to relinquish territory. That would change, however, if the US were to annex it. Besides fighting for their new state, Americans under the newly elected President Polk were seeking to bring to fruition the idea of Manifest Destiny. The Louisiana Purchase had helped to make this closer to reality during Thomas Jefferson's presidency, but the US was now eyeing Mexican territory in an effort to fulfill what they thought was right and inevitable.

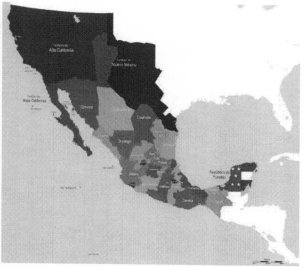

Mexico in 1845: In the Path of US Expansion
https://commons.wikimedia.org/wiki/File:Mapa_Mexico_1845.PNG

Initially, there was not much support on either side of the border for a war. However, Mexico was in a much weaker position: they were still attempting to build a nation amid civil wars and other power struggles. The US had been a nation for several decades and had coalesced around a strong central government. The odds were stacked against Mexico.

By annexing Texas, the US proved that it was finally willing to take over Mexican lands. After the annexation, the US began to claim ownership of lands that were still in dispute. Prior to gaining Texas, the US had sent John Slidell and a small contingent of politicians to Mexico to negotiate the purchase of a large swath of the northern area of Mexico. The US wanted to replicate the cheap cost of the Louisiana Purchase, which had more than doubled the size of the US in 1803 for fifteen million dollars (or eighteen dollars per square mile). Slidell was authorized to offer thirty million dollars for the region, but the Mexican government would not even meet with him, as they had no desire to sell the lands.

When Slidell returned saying that Mexico was unwilling to meet with him, President Polk decided to market it as an insult to the nation. Polk then forced a war with Mexico because he believed it was the only way to potentially acquire the lands he believed were destined to be a part of the United States. To ensure that the US military would instigate a war, he sent troops to reside in the disputed region south of the Texas border. These troops were technically invading another nation, and unsurprisingly, Mexico fired on them. This was exactly what Polk wanted. By spinning the invasion by the US into a story about the death of a US soldier on US lands at the hands of Mexicans, Polk finally created the excuse he needed to start a war to steal land from Mexico. He deceived the American people when he said that Mexico had "invaded our territory and shed American blood upon American soil." He then ordered Congress to declare war. Many Americans questioned this. Northern states said that Polk, who was a Southerner, was attempting to acquire more slave-holding states and give greater control to them. There were also many Americans who simply did not want to go to war to steal lands from another country, for it had been less than one hundred years since they had won their own freedom. Many people still felt strongly that the US should not be an aggressor (except when it came to displacing the Native Americans). Despite the protests of many Americans, Congress gave their approval on May 13th, 1846.

The Mexican-American War

The Mexican-American War would later be described by a young second lieutenant named Ulysses S. Grant as a war that was "one of the most unjust ever waged by a stronger against a weaker nation. It was an instance of a republic following the bad example of European monarchies, in not considering justice in their desire to acquire additional territory." This was exactly what had made many Americans oppose the idea of war before it was declared. However, once they were committed, many Americans felt it was necessary to provide support and boost the morale of the soldiers. Even if the war was wrong, the Americans did not blame the soldiers. The Mexicans, on the other hand, were not only against the war but also not in the position to benefit from it. America was now an aggressor that had largely been at peace since winning its independence, in stark contrast to the chaotic aftermath of the Mexican War of Independence. Mexican morale was already low, and this was yet another fight, but this time against a much more powerful force. The Mexican soldiers and people were as aware as Ulysses S. Grant of the superiority of the US forces.

Three notable officers fought in the Mexican-American War: General Zachary Taylor, Ulysses S. Grant, and Robert E. Lee. This was both Grant and Lee's first experience fighting in a war. Despite the novice US commanders and the superior numbers of the Mexicans, the Americans managed to quickly rule the battlefield.

The Mexican-American War began in April 1846 with 8,000 American soldiers. Wanting to provide support and fight for their country, more than 60,000 Americans soon joined as volunteers. There were over 73,000 Mexicans, who were also a mix of regular soldiers and volunteers. The Mexican Navy couldn't contend with the much more robust US Navy. But annexing Texas was not enough: Manifest Destiny had to be fulfilled. To further undermine Mexico, Polk sowed discontent in the other Mexican territories of modern-day California by sending John Fremont and Stephen Kearny to instigate a revolution in the area. Thus, the people in California declared themselves the Bear Flag Republic even before they learned of the fighting between Mexico and the US. Led by Fremont, they marched on a military outpost, a Mexican presidio, and secured the region for the US. While Fremont was ensuring the theft of the California territory, Kearny was enacting a similar strategy in New Mexico, driving the governor out of the region. He and his band captured the capital, and after their success, Kearny led his men west to join with the successful Californians.

As Kearny and Fremont secured the northern region, Generals Zachary Taylor and Winfield Scott marched on Mexico City. Taylor faced Antonio López de Santa Anna directly and headed toward the capital's center while Scott approached the city from a different direction. Scott and his men successfully took control of the city, leaving the Mexicans with no option but to surrender in September of 1847. This put the US in a better position to negotiate for land at a much lower cost.

Ironically, the annexation of Texas and the Mexican-American War would be two major contributing factors to the American Civil War. By pushing for something that most Americans did not want, the nation became even more bitterly divided. Discussions about Polk's underhanded methods and unconstitutional behavior in essentially forcing the country into an unjustified war became widespread. One of the nation's most notable writers of the time, Henry David Thoreau, believed so strongly that the war was wrong that he was arrested for refusing to pay taxes in protest of the war. His protests begat *Civil Disobedience*, an essay that is still used today to enact peaceful change.

These events were all a prelude for what would come later. The acquisition of so much land by a nation that was already so divided would result in far more internal hostilities. By winning the Mexican-American War, the US all but assured that it would tear itself apart just a couple of decades later. The Missouri Compromise of 1850, which was meant to address the question of whether the new

American lands would be slave states or free states, would ultimately be the undoing of the US for many years.

Treaty of Guadalupe Hidalgo

It is also ironic that the treaty to end the war was made without the president's knowledge. Signed on February 2nd, 1848, the treaty set the boundaries for the regions that would be a part of the US going forward, including all the southwestern states of the US today.

Lands Lost after the Mexican-American War

Kballen, CC BY-SA 3.0 <http://creativecommons.org/licenses/by-sa/3.0/>, via Wikimedia Commons https://commons.wikimedia.org/wiki/File:Mexican_Cession.png

Mexico received nearly half the money that had been offered to them prior to the war, with all this land becoming a part of the US for between fifteen and eighteen million dollars (the US also took on some of the Mexican debt for these regions, increasing the total cost of the lands). The disputed lands with Texas (shown in the previous chapter) were identified, and new borders were drawn. A single war lost Mexico over half of its total land. Polk endorsed the treaty, then sent it to Congress for final approval. It passed by a vote of 34 to 14 in March 1848.

There was a sense of victory in the US following the completion of what it believed to be inevitable Manifest Destiny. However, the results of the war further widened the divide between abolitionists and slave owners. While it was inevitable that the slavery issue would need to be resolved, the addition of so much new territory and no ability to ensure that slavery did not spread into the territories where it was banned would force a struggle that soon became open warfare.

Chapter 9 – Role in the Civil War

Texas had finally achieved what many of the American settlers had expected on December 29, 1845. Had the settlers better understood the tensions in the US, they likely would have decided against seeking entry as a state. The US was moving in the same direction as Mexico: slavery was quickly becoming untenable to most Americans. While Texas fell firmly on the pro-slavery side, the South was significantly outnumbered by the North in terms of population.

The fears of US Congress members who had wanted to avoid annexing Texas because of the unbalance it would likely cause in the current unrest proved to be well-founded in 1861. Many Texans were much more inclined to find a peaceful resolution with the northern states than they had been with Mexico, but they were unwilling to compromise when it came to retaining their slaves. There were other concerns, such as the fear that northerners would force their views on southern states, but ultimately it was the fear of the slaveholders that drove Texas to join the other southern states in seceding from the nation they had joined less than two decades earlier. Though the primary battles occurred in the eastern states, Texas did have a significant role to play in the American Civil War.

The Election of Abraham Lincoln and the Texas Convention to Address Secession

Many of the southern states were unsettled by the election of Abraham Lincoln to the presidency. In November of 1860, Sam Houston was the Texas governor, and he had worked hard for the annexation of Texas. Despite his misgivings for the direction the US was taking, he was unwilling to do anything that would jeopardize the state's place in the country. As Texans called for their governor to hold a convention to discuss the state's next moves, Houston refused. He knew that they were going to discuss the possibility of secession, and he would not do anything to support such an action. When South Carolina seceded in December of 1860, other southern states were holding their own conventions to discuss following South Carolina's example.

A group of prominent Texans, including Oran M. Roberts, George M. Flournoy, and John S. Ford, formed a group to force the discussion. They wanted to hold a convention in the early part of January 1861. To thwart the convention, Houston called for a special legislative session that he hoped would reject any recognition of the convention. The session was held, but it did not go as Houston had hoped. Instead of refusing to acknowledge the convention, the legislature approved it with the stipulation that the people of Texas would get a final vote on its outcome.

The convention began on January 28, 1861, ironically meeting in Austin, Texas. Had Stephen Austin still been alive, he probably would have opposed the move, yet they were meeting in the capital city named after him to undo one of the last major fights he had engaged in—joining the US. Most of the people who attended the convention were in favor of secession, and the ordinance was adopted on February 1st. The final vote in favor of secession was 166 to 8, and it was approved. Following the successful passage of secession, the convention met again to make the final declaration that they were leaving the US to join the Confederate States of American.

Houston refused to acknowledge the decisions of the convention and would not take an oath to what he saw as the illegal and treasonous turning on the US. Consequently, Houston was deposed as Governor. They then filled the position with Edward Clark, the Lieutenant Governor.

Lincoln was sworn into office on March 4, 1861, and to support Houston's resistance to the secession, he told the legendary leader that he was willing to send troops to Texas. However, Houston's anger at the secession of Texas did not mean that he was willing to incite violence within the state. To reduce the violence and threat of a civil war within the state, Houston retired and moved to Huntsville, Texas. He did not live to see the end of the war, as he died in Huntsville in 1863, a year before the war ended.

Movement to Take Control of Federal Lands and Supplies

As the convention was preparing to take its next steps, the committee sent troops to remove the US army from Texas. The Confederate troops first went to confront Major General David E. Twiggs, who commanded the American troops in Texas. He quickly agreed to surrender and remove nearly 3,000 Union soldiers who were currently working around the state, including in the frontier. After the Union soldiers left, Confederate troops occupied the many shelters and fortifications around the frontiers of the state.

While Texas soldiers wanted to contribute to the war, Texans understood they could not simply abandon the frontiers. If their people were left unprotected, sentiment could easily shift against the elitists who focused on fighting the US instead of protecting their own citizens. Even though just over 46,000 Texans voted for secession, nearly 15,000 people had voted against it.

The state had a large German population who were very much against the move, and they formed what came to be known as the Union Loyalty League. Their presence, along with Texans who were loyal to the US, was sizeable enough that violence within the state required the government to declare martial law in regions with high loyalist populations. Others sought to leave Texas to live in the US, particularly those who were born in the north and had migrated to Texas following its annexation.

The Confederates were vicious in trying to put down any Union sentiment or loyalty. For example, they tried and executed the US loyalist Josefa "Chipita" Rodriguez, claiming with no supporting evidence that she had killed a traveler, John Savage. Union loyalists who tried to leave were often hunted down and killed.

When the year ended, 25,000 Texans had joined the fledgling Confederate States Army. An estimated two-thirds were cavalrymen, in large part because their experiences in the frontier made them adept horsemen.

The Drawn-out War

Initially, the Confederacy seemed to be doing very well against the Union. However, it was ultimately a war of attrition, with most of the battles occurring in southern states. The fervor that the southern states felt in the beginning helped to bolster several critical wins. Ultimately, the Confederacy had to win the war quickly to remain their own nation, though. The US army was not as familiar with the lands where the fighting occurred, which was another advantage to the Confederacy. As the war moved into a second and then a third year, it became obvious that the Union had all the critical advantages to conduct a longer war. They had a much larger population, which meant that troops were not pushed to the same limits as Confederate troops. The perpetual fighting hampered and then began to break the enthusiasm that had boosted the South in the beginning. The North also had a significant advantage in terms of resources. Most of the nation's manufacturing and resource production occurred in the North, while the South was predominantly agricultural. As many of the battles occurred in the South, food production was interrupted and crops destroyed, reducing even this resource for the southern army.

Texas was not affected nearly as much as the southeastern states because it was not as critical as states such as Virginia and Georgia to winning the war. If the most important states in the Confederacy could be brought down, Texas would have no recourse but to accept defeat. It would have been interesting to have seen what would have happened to Texas had they either not joined the US in 1845 or seceded to become their own nation instead of joining the rest of the South in the Confederacy. The US would not have been able to fight both the Confederacy and Texas, which would have given Texas four years to fortify themselves against war with the US. It is uncertain whether the US would have been willing to re-enter another war after four years of fighting against the Confederacy.

Since Texas did tie themselves to the Confederacy, they were not immune to attacks by Union soldiers. It is estimated that 70,000 to 90,000 Texans joined the Confederate Army over the years. At least thirty-seven Texans held prominent roles in the Confederate Army, as well. The only two major battles after Texas' secession that did not include Texans were First Manassas and Chancellorsville.

One population that had been growing since the Texas Revolution were Mexican Americans. Mexicans had joined the American settlers during that war, and many Mexicans fled the political upheaval and uncertainty of Mexico, choosing to live in Texas. They were often the targets of extreme racism, even by the law enforcement agency of Texas Rangers. With a large population of Mexican Americans not willing to leave the US to become a nation that was attempting to perpetuate institutional racism through slavery, there were soon significant fights between Texans and Mexican Americans. Both sides sought to recruit the large Mexican American demographic. Since many Americans had married Mexicans, the lines were not as well established, though, and about 2,550 Mexican Americans decided to help the Confederacy. However, nearly 1,000 joined the Union, a much higher percentage than any other demographic who were unhappy with the departure of Texas from the US.

Most Texas soldiers remained in Texas to fight Union soldiers trying to infiltrate Texas. One of the reasons why so many soldiers remained in Texas was that the Union was not the only enemy that Texans faced. Though their numbers had been significantly reduced, there were still many Native Americans who were taking advantage of the American Civil War to attack settlers on the frontier, most notably the Comanches. Mexicans were also turning the Civil War to their advantage, with many raiders attacking settlements and towns in the southern parts of the state.

Western Texas became a place of refuge for deserters from both sides of the war, outlaws, and settlers who sought protection after abandoning their homes because of Native American raids. This strange combination of different groups of people was a major reason Texas is associated with the Wild West. As there was little military presence in the western part of the state, these groups created their own set of laws (or failed to make any), and lawlessness was rampant. It was impossible for Texas to protect such a large area, so they chose to fight the Union to the north and east, and Mexicans to the south. The west was largely left to its own devices and became a region where many outlaws made their home.

Despite the lack of any real protection from the Texas military in the west, the Confederacy wanted to expand into the west, at least in the beginning of the war. Initially, the Confederacy succeeded, as the US did not have an adequate military presence in these territories. The Texans accomplished a measure of success as they pushed into the New Mexico territory, which was part of the Union. This victory was quickly stymied, then put down, as the US took control of the supply chains. The Union also mobilized soldiers located in California, resulting in the withdrawal of the Confederacy from the western regions they had claimed.

Another problem that Texas faced that the other southern states did not was a dearth of railroads. As a massive state that was still new to the US, there had not been adequate time to build the kinds of intricate railroad systems that were needed to supply the many different outposts. Having to rely on stagecoaches quickly proved problematic for the Texas Confederates, as the Union could easily interrupt and stop their supply chains. Keeping their ports open in the Gulf of Mexico was important, and, initially, Texas was successful there. Then the US sent superior and better-equipped ships to take control of the critical port in Galveston, Texas—the largest seaport in Texas—which they needed for the supplies that arrived from other Confederate states and nations. The Union managed to take control of the port in October 1862, but the Confederates recaptured it just after New Year's Day in 1863. Despite the Confederacy's success at reclaiming Galveston, the Union had established and maintained a blockade, which became more robust every month. Initially, the blockade did not appear to be very successful as ships slipped through several times a week. But, as the Union wore down the other southern states, they could focus more on the Gulf Coast to prevent supplies from moving freely.

Ironically, Texas ended up turning to Mexico for resources. With tensions still very high (it wasn't even twenty years since the revolution), Texans resorted to smuggling goods across the border, as Mexico had no reason to provide them with any substantial support. Still, Mexico was willing to trade for cotton, and it didn't hurt for Mexico to help both sides. After all, they had as much reason to loathe the US as Texas. Keeping the fight going could both provide them with extra resources and weaken their northern neighbors.

The longer the war dragged on, the more ordinary life changed in Texas, even in areas that were far from conflict with Mexico and Native Americans. Food production was increasingly rationed because such a large portion was required for the soldiers. Slaveholders also moved from other states into Texas, which saw a rise in the number of slaves from 182,000 to 230,000, largely because Texas was far less affected by the war than the other states. This put free African Americans in peril because slave owners did not respect the fact that they were free and would often force them into slavery. Many left the state as a result.

End of the War

Texas contributed many soldiers to fight the Union, but ultimately, the Confederacy could not win a long war. Their only real hope of winning was to win quickly. On April 9, 1865, General Robert E. Lee signed the Confederate surrender, and the next month saw the surrender of other Confederate departments.

As it became clear that the war was ending, Texas Governor Pendleton Murrah tried to ease the transition by issuing three different proclamations:

> 1. He ordered all Texas civil officers to keep control of all public property.
>
> 2. He requested a special legislative session.
>
> 3. He called for the election of new delegates for a new convention.

Unfortunately, his proclamations were too little, too late. Confederate soldiers had already begun to disband because they had not been paid for months, and it was clear that they weren't going to be paid. As they left, the soldiers took whatever they could. Chaos and disorder quickly spread, as soldiers started to follow their basic instincts to survive over all else.

This was not the biggest concern for men like Murrah, though. Those who had served in prominent positions in the Confederacy were facing serious charges and repercussions for treason as the war ended. Opting to flee instead of face the consequences, many of the most prominent people in Texas left the state to save themselves. This meant that there were far too few leaders in the state at a time when it desperately needed them. Following the assassination of President Lincoln in April of 1865, President Andrew Johnson was faced with having to help rebuild all the southern states while trying to establish himself as a leader. Johnson finally appointed a new government for the state of Texas in June, and he chose A. J. Hamilton, a former Texas congressman in the US legislature. Until Hamilton's arrival, a Union soldier, General Granger, oversaw Texas, and one of his first actions was to declare that Texas slaves were now free. Today, Texas still celebrates June 19th as Emancipation Day.

One of the first things that Governor Hamilton did was to call for all loyal men to join in a convention in Austin to discuss the future of the state. Based on what President Johnson had instructed, Hamilton was seeking to establish a new government as quickly as possible and restore the relationship between the state and federal government. Texas would not be allowed to govern itself for almost a decade.

Chapter 10 – Reconstruction

For the first time, the people of Texas lost their bid for something they wanted, showing just how much different being a part of the US was compared to being a part of Mexico. The US was older, better established, and even during the Civil War, they had established agreements with other nations that helped to push them forward. Now those same people were responsible for the future of the state. Texas had lost its heroes from the Texas Revolution, and those who had pushed them into seceding had fled. While Governor Hamilton had represented Texas in the US Congress, he could be considered disconnected from the state after four years of war.

Like the rest of the former Confederate states, Texas experienced a serious economic upheaval and shift in its workforce. Plantations and ranchers no longer had free labor, and there was fear of the resentment that may occur now that African Americans were free. People who had once held sway over the state found themselves with far less power. The state had to learn to evolve and navigate an uncertain future.

Arrival of US Forces

With the end of the war, the US began sending troops into southern states, which meant the recent enemies of Texas were controlling the state. The forces began to arrive in May 1865, making Texans very uncomfortable. Each of the commanders who entered the state had their own idea of what they were to do in Texas, though most of them believed their first job was to ensure the freedom of former slaves and make sure their rights weren't violated. There was also a strong sentiment that the people of Texas should remain under military control until they had proved they were once again loyal to the US. The commanders didn't agree on what would prove that people were loyal, which could have led to decades of military occupation. This would clearly not make the people feel like they were part of the country, but more like prisoners in the US. Fortunately, the US military could not spare numerous soldiers to any single state for long, so the fears that the military would interfere in the Texas economy would prove to be unfounded.

Initially, 51,000 soldiers were sent to Texas, but a year after the end of the war, that number diminished to 3,000. Just as before the war, many of those soldiers were stationed near the frontier to protect the people from the same threats they had been facing from the Native Americans and Mexican raiders. The military was unable to enact much change across the state because they simply did not have the number to enforce the laws.

The Founding of the Freedmen's Bureau and Expressed Interests by Former Slaves

Of greater concern to the old power structure in Texas was the creation of the Bureau of Refugees, Freedmen, and Abandoned Lands, better known as the Freedmen's Bureau. The Bureau was formed under the control of Major General Edgar M. Gregory. Beginning in September of 1865, the Bureau managed the oversight of any events or actions that pertained to freedmen, refugees, and lands that had been abandoned, usually by Confederate officials or representatives who fled. Its most time-consuming and important task was ensuring that the former slaves could transition into life as free men. Gregory quickly showed that he would take a much more conservative approach to how this should happen, making it easier for the older Texan families to feel comfortable with his actions. His approach was usually to force former slaves to return to the lands that they had previously worked and resume the same work they had once done. To keep them on these lands, the Bureau often forced former slaves to sign contracts that would require them to work there at a stipulated wage. It was almost impossible for former slaves to fight this since they had no way of acquiring lands on their own. Just as they had done when Mexico banned slaves, the plantation and ranch owners used debt servitude to make it all but impossible for most slaves to leave because they were not paid enough. Essentially, they would have to pay for the places where they had been forced to live as slaves, which would leave little to no money left of the wages that they earned.

Texans wound up pleased with the way Gregory ensured that laborers were plentiful and that there was minimal economic impact on the wealthy landowners. What he implemented that upset many white Texans was the effort to educate the former slaves. White Texans were further angered by what they considered interference in how their judicial systems treated African Americans. These criticisms were common, but the reality was likely far less impactful than the complaints implied. The US government did not have adequate funds to provide substantial education to the recently freed people, nor did it have enough personnel to significantly protect the freedmen. It is likely that the Texans were simply complaining because they believed that their power had been reduced, not about any noticeable changes. The people were more concerned with potential changes to the status quo than what was accomplished during the first couple of years.

The biggest threat came from the freedmen themselves. Having been given their freedom, former slaves wanted to have the same opportunities as their white counterparts. From pushing for education to wanting to control their own work schedule, freed slaves were pressing for rights to be guaranteed to all people in the US. This was the most obvious threat to the former slave owners, as well as those who had never had enough money to own slaves. The freedmen could work for less, or so it was thought, which meant that it would be harder for white people to find jobs. The freedmen wanting to control their schedules and living conditions was considered a burden to the people who used to own and control all aspects of their slaves' lives. White Texans began to openly oppose the push to improve the lives of former slaves, often resorting to threats or violence. In response, the freedmen demanded that the US provide legal protections against the offenders. They began a coordinated effort to petition for protection, meeting in Austin on March 10, 1866. The conference resulted in representatives demanding voting protections and that the state provide public lands for education. From this meeting, the Austin Freedman's Society formed, which would become the core of the African American Republican Party.

A False Start at Returning to the US as a State

President Johnson set the rules that would allow Confederate states to return to the US. All the states were put under the control of an appointed governor who would oversee the states' progress in meeting those requirements. The initial work for governors had three parts: governors ensured that the act of secession implemented in all southern states was nullified, initiated and enforced the abolishment of slavery, and repudiated the debt accrued by all the Confederate states.

For the most part, the way governors implemented the changes was intended to help restore the states' legislatures. Conventions were held, and the delegates who participated were required to take the oath of amnesty. Only voters who had also taken the oath could elect delegates. They then ratified the decisions that were passed by the delegates during the convention and would be allowed to elect their own governor, legislature, and officials. Once repopulated by representatives who had sworn to be loyal to the US, the state legislatures would have to ratify the 13th Amendment, which abolished slavery in the US.

With the arrival of Governor Hamilton, many of the Union supporters either returned to the state or found themselves in a position of control. This was one intention behind the requirements for restored statehood: the president was looking to prevent the old antebellum leaders from having any say in the direction their states would take. The president and other US leaders knew that allowing the antebellum leaders to continue to have a voice would not only jeopardize the return of the states into the Union but also prevent the full abolishment of slavery. Their exclusion from power ensured minimal issues in restoring the states to the US.

Hamilton was not as effective as some of the other appointed governors, and he was unable to prevent the previous leaders from gaining considerable power within Texas. The election of January 8, 1866, saw the state's old power dynamics largely resumed. This was possible because these leaders had not lost much of their economic control over the states and had hindered others from rising to power. When the Texas convention was held in February of 1866, many of the leaders were the same as those who had agreed to secession. Because of this, there were many more concessions made between the two sides. In the end, Texas did only the minimum to return to the US as a state. The convention quickly passed many of the laws enacted during the war that were not in direct violation of the US Constitution.

Forcing out the Antebellum Leaders

The problem with Texas' return to the US became clear when the Texas legislature refused to ratify either the 13th or 14th Amendments. To further insult the requirements, the legislature passed what were called "black codes" that dictated how freedmen could work within the state, giving most of the control to the antebellum leaders. The Unionists in the state quickly decided that the people in power were not only unrepentant for the war they had caused but also determined not to abide by the requirements to return to the country.

Consequently, none of the elected officials were permitted to assume their roles in Washington, D.C. Nor was Texas the only state that proved it had learned almost nothing from the Civil War.

Because of the difficulties encountered during the first few years after the Civil War, the US Congress passed the First Reconstruction Act. This required the states that had seceded from the Union to be divided into different military districts controlled by the US military. Texas was a part of the Fifth Military District under this new law. Governor James Throckmorton was removed from office by General Griffin, who became manager of the district in March of 1867. Griffin died a few months later from the yellow fever epidemic and was succeeded by Joseph Reynolds. Reynolds pushed for the implementation of reforms Griffin had intended to make, including several special orders that removed many of the elected state officials from their positions—including over 400 county officials, the city officials who were elected in San Antonio, and most of the officials in Austin. Reynolds appointed people whom he trusted or who were known to be loyal to the US and had completed the Congress "Ironclad Test Oath," which required officials to swear that they had never taken up arms against the US. This excluded nearly all the antebellum leaders, ensuring they were not able to return to power. Considering the size of the state, it was nearly impossible for Reynolds to oversee all the positions, so he had others manage positions on the local level. Officials who could not pass the test would be considered incapable of holding their positions. As of April 25, 1869, all the positions held by unqualified personnel were considered vacant.

The First Reconstruction Act created further steps that all former Confederate states had to take before they would be able to send representatives to the US government. Another convention was held, and it was decided that the only individuals not able to become officials were women and felons. Any man who was at least twenty-one years old and had not been convicted of a felony could be a delegate, even a former slave. The convention would dictate that a new constitution be written for each former Confederate state, and each state would have to ratify the 13th and 14th Amendments. Only then would the US Congress consider readmission of that state into the Union.

Conservatives in Texas decided not to vote, hoping to deny a majority vote for what was to come. Because of their refusal to vote (even though many had registered), the radical Republicans easily carried a majority. The convention was held from June 1, 1868, to February 1869.

Whereas most former Confederate states had to contend with opportunists who used the devastation from the war to enrich themselves during reconstruction, Texas had a largely unique problem. Because of how expansive the state is, lawlessness was a significant problem except in the major cities and large towns. There were many outlaws who could easily escape the laws as the state tried to draft a new constitution. This would be a residual problem long after Texas was returned to the Union.

Chapter 11 – Texas Rangers – One of the Most Illustrious Law Enforcement Agencies

When Moses Morrison asked for volunteers to protect settlers, he could not have imagined how instrumental that group would become, eventually evolving into the law enforcement agency known as the Texas Rangers. From their humble beginnings, the Texas Rangers would go through many different changes, and not always for the better, eventually becoming one of the most well-known agencies in the US. Though not the oldest law enforcement agency (that distinction goes to the US Marshals Service), the Texas Rangers have become one of the most well-respected institutions, with their agents helping even other states to bring criminals to justice.

Original Role of the Rangers

The first Texas Rangers were not a part of any official organization. Volunteers who heeded the call in 1823, they doubled when Austin decided that more men were needed. With so many different people in the region, the original group of Rangers were as diverse as the populations who settled in Texas. There were frontiersmen who had learned how to live on the fringes of society, Native Americans who knew the region and wildlife, and a few members with considerable knowledge of guns. They were adept trackers, hunters, horse riders, and gunmen. They modified guns to make weapons that were ahead of their time. Yet these men largely worked for the greater good. Most of the time they worked well together, and their unique skills made the volunteer group one of the most effective protectors in Texas.

The Rangers would go on to fill similar roles over the years, protecting settlers during the War for Independence, as well as intimidating Mexicans who killed settlers. While their roles were largely as protectors instead of law enforcement officers for the first few decades, most of that would change once Texas became its own country.

Making Their Own Rules

With the new nation of Texas having little cohesion and few laws in place, the Texas Rangers started to operate by their own rules. Their primary role was to fight raiding Native Americans, but they soon lost sight of that, going against orders to drive Native Americans from their lands. They would also take a very aggressive approach against Mexicans, especially when they uncovered plots in which bandits sought to sow discontentment in the new nation.

Over time, the Rangers gained a reputation as protectors, and their aggression against other populations was welcome—largely seen as protective of the people. After Texas was annexed to the US, the Rangers would encounter fewer Mexicans trying to sow discord and had already successfully driven Native Americans from areas near settlements in most places.

Now there were fewer enemies, but the Rangers had come to expect a certain amount of respect and control wherever they went and soon began to use those aggressive tactics on Americans. It was only then that most of the people began to turn on the Rangers. While the sentiment had been building near the end of the 19th century, by the early 20th century, most citizens had taken a much dimmer view of the Texas Rangers. For the next several decades, the group was viewed as a growing threat because of their cocky attitudes and lack of regard for the laws. Texans began to criticize them for resorting to violence before negotiating, a tactic that the Rangers had been using for decades without being questioned—until it was used against Texans.

It would take several more decades (roughly around the time of World War II) and a few highly reputable members to finally restore the Rangers to a place of honor and respect.

A Remarkable Record Against Notorious Criminals

Some of the loss of respect for the Rangers was unjustified, partly because they went after criminals who were considered heroes. One of the most notable criminals they captured was Sam Bass, a bandit who operated during the 1880s. The people loved him because he and his outlaws targeted the rich, and he often spent his money freely with the lower classes. Because of this, the people were angry when the Rangers finally caught up with Bass in July of 1887. During a shootout, he and his men managed to escape, but Bass had been shot by one of the Rangers. Bass would die the next day, July, 21st 1887, while in Ranger custody. This proved to the Texas legislature that the Rangers were still a formidable and necessary force. The Rangers initially gained the respect of the politicians, even if the people were unhappy with the way the Rangers had acted. Though Sam Bass was considered a hero, his band had not killed just the rich or those protecting their money: civilians had been killed, as well. The Rangers' use of force could be justified because Bass and his men would often shoot as soon as they knew law enforcement had found them.

The next infamous criminal that the Rangers tracked was John Wesley Hardin. They successfully captured him, but the legal system allowed this notorious criminal and murderer to be released under the guise of being rehabilitated. He then became a lawyer who hired others to kill for him. The Rangers did not track him again, largely because Hardin got sloppy after "going straight." When he failed to pay one of his assassins, the assassin killed him in a bar. The Rangers had not killed him, but they had done everything in their power to control this dangerous criminal who did not have the support of the people.

The most well-known criminals that the Rangers took down were Bonnie Elizabeth Parker and Clyde Champion Barrow, better known today as Bonnie and Clyde. Like Bass, they were criminals who were heroes to the people. Bonnie and Clyde did not help the people, but they operated during the Great Depression. Their ability to take from the rich to improve their own situation was admired by those who had no way to make a living. When they were ambushed and killed on May 23, 1934, their deaths were met with a mix of sadness and interest. They may not have helped the people, but they had done something to improve their own lot. Some civilians were killed because of them, which was partly why they were not mourned the same way Bass was mourned. Their notoriety is more closely aligned today with that of serial killers: their actions are considered wrong and immoral, but people cannot help but be fascinated by them.

These are some of the most notable cases the Rangers helped resolve, proving they had evolved into a law-abiding agency that could get difficult jobs done. Today they are a highly respected agency at the forefront of law enforcement agencies in the US. They help other agencies around the country resolve cases and review cold cases as new technologies evolve. One of the most notable cases they helped resolve recently was the murder of Irene Garza in April 1960. Though it took over 50 years, the Rangers were finally able to prove that she was murdered by a retired priest in 2016. Based on the evidence submitted by the Rangers and other members of law enforcement, Father John Feit was convicted of her murder and given a life sentence. This likely would not have been possible without the Rangers' dedication and constant review of the evidence and forensic techniques to finally see that justice was done.

Chapter 12 – Texas Tea – The Texas Oil Boom

As the state recovered from the economic devastation of the Civil War, a discovery was made that drew thousands of people in a hunt for riches. The state was not rich in gold, but by the end of the 19th century, there was a resource that had come to be more valuable to Americans than gold: Texas was rich in oil. The discovery in the small town of Corsicana would quickly transform it into a major industrial center. While oil had been found in Nacogdoches County back in 1866, the finding in Corsicana would begin to change the economy of the entire state.

An Accidental Find

When the American Well and Prospecting Company began drilling in Corsicana, they were interested in finding water. Instead of hitting water on June 9, 1894, they struck oil. The Corsicana City Council, which had hired them, paid only half of the agreed-upon fee because the company had not found the water they needed.

The initial production filled two and a half barrels a day, which was enough to attract plenty of attention to the region. Oil prospectors began drilling for other wells, hoping to find the rich deposits suggested by the initial find. The second well ended up being dry, but the next one, drilled in May 1896, provided a much higher yield than the first, filling over twenty barrels every day. About six months later, forty-seven wells had been drilled, and they produced nearly 66,000 barrels a day. To better handle the unexpected amount of oil, the first Texas oil refinery was built in 1897. This significantly increased how much oil could be pulled from the land, and 287 wells ensured that the refinery remained busy over the next few decades.

The American Well Prospecting Company began to focus on drilling oil, making its owners rich off both the oil they were putting into barrels and the technology they devised to better drill for oil. Seeing others come to the town with the hopes of finding oil, the company created a complementary business that repaired the devices used to pump oil. The company profited from the oil production and their unique understanding of how to drill for it (knowledge that was not as widespread since the only other place where oil and gas were mined with such fervor was in Pennsylvania). The company also developed the hydraulic rotary drilling rig and secured rights to the invention in 1900. This would be the rig that was used for a much larger oil discovery in 1901.

With the discovery of oil, Corsicana experienced a boom and an influx of financial wealth. The town had a new courthouse built in 1905, and its chamber of commerce was established in 1917.

The Lucas Gusher

The first major oil find was in Corsicana, but it was Spindletop that would cause the largest oil boom in Texas. On January 10, 1901, the mining engineer Captain A. F. Lucas was drilling in Spindletop when the ground shook, followed by an eruption from the drill site. Oil gushed up into the air like an exploding volcano, but with black liquid instead of lava. It was impossible to stop this outpouring, and thousands of barrels were released into the air and poured over the ground before the engineers were finally able to stem the flow. This dramatic eruption attracted a lot of attention from across the country, convincing many that there was a real chance of becoming rich by drilling in Texas. The event has often been replayed in movies and TV because of the incredible visual effect.

The Lucas Gusher significantly increased how much oil Texas produced, bringing the total number of barrels produced a year from just under 840,000 to nearly 4.4 million barrels by the end of 1901. Over the course of 1902, the small region of Spindletop saw the production of over 17.4 million barrels, which was over 94% of the oil produced in Texas that year. It also dropped the cost for a barrel of oil to just $0.03 per barrel.

A Second and Third Find in Corsicana

As drilling continued for the next fifteen years, the oil craze eventually began to settle down since, based on the amount of oil in the region, it seemed like production had stabilized. Then another deposit was found in 1923, and it caused a frenzy. During this time, known as the Roaring 20s, most of America was feeling positive about the economy, and many people were prospering. Seeing an opportunity to further improve their financial situations, people flocked to Texas in the thousands hoping to strike it rich. The fervor and drive resembled the handful of historic gold rushes that had caused people to uproot their families and stream west, but a much larger investment was required to drill for oil than to pan for gold.

Corsicana had once had an economy that was based on agriculture and shipping, but with each boom, the town changed. Following the first major oil boom, the town expanded far beyond any expectation. By the end of the second boom, it had become an industrial center and hub of oil production in the US. Many businesses grew up around the flocks of people who sought riches, largely to their detriment, as individuals could not reach the biggest deposits.

Due to the two major oil booms, Corsicana had become the wealthiest town in Texas. According to one reporter in 1956, more than twenty millionaires resided in Corsicana, with most of them making their fortune through the oil deposits, whether directly or indirectly (whether making repairs, selling goods, or building in the area). Later that year, a third deposit was found, and an additional 500 wells were drilled around Corsicana. There were so many drills and wells that one person described the sight of Corsicana as there being a drill in almost every person's backyard. By the end of the 1950s, more than 125 million barrels of oil had been collected in Corsicana.

The events over the span of sixty years significantly changed the history and economy of not only Corsicana but all of Texas. Without the first discovery of oil in the town, the rig used for the Lucas Gusher would likely have been less efficient, resulting in a much less dramatic finding.

The people of Corsicana continue to celebrate their good fortune every year at the Derrick Days Festival.

Timing Was Everything

One of the reasons that Texas gained so much attention for its oil deposits was the timing. The Native Americans had known about oil centuries before any of the Europeans arrived and had used it for medicinal purposes (though it is not entirely clear how they used it). The Spanish explorers had various uses for it, but primarily as a way of caulking leaks in their vessels. Until the 19th century, oil was not used as a primary transportation fuel. The combustion engine was first invented toward the end of the 18th century, but people did not realize its full potential until nearly 100 years later, with the advent of the first motor vehicles to use one. By 1886, motor vehicles were being produced with internal combustion engines, and the potential for oil to change the world began to increase the demand for the substance.

Because motor vehicles were not yet something that many people owned, the potential for this use of the oil was not recognized by the people of Texas who had hired well drillers. However, the American Well Prospecting Company that struck oil was very forward-thinking for the time and knew they stood to make a considerable profit from what they had found. Had they struck oil a few decades earlier, the finding would have been ignored, just like the first people who struck oil in Nacogdoches County. Ultimately, it was the timing of the find that would change the trajectory of drilling in the state.

Drilling would begin to occur in many places across Texas. Some of it was focused on finding water, but many people were hoping to strike oil. Offshore drilling began during 1908 near the island of Galveston, in the Galveston Bay. Initially, the drilling was unsuccessful, and many people gave up, leaving the field abandoned. In 1916, a gusher was found in the region, and many people moved there hoping that it was as rich in oil as Spindletop and Corsicana. When the people who managed W. T. Waggoner Ranch tried to drill for water on their lands in Wichita County in 1911, they encounter oil. This was one of four oil fields that would be established in the region. Oil was soon discovered at the Ranger Field in 1917 and Burkburnett townsite in 1918. The Texas oil boom was in full swing by the beginning of the Roaring 20s, and because of the changes in technology, the substance became incredibly valuable.

The biggest oil discoveries were in the eastern part of the state, in what is called the East Texas Oil Field. The oil in the region was found in October of 1930 by C. M. Joiner. The discovery was entirely unexpected, as the fields had already been condemned by geologists hired by major companies to find oil. Because of the find, many people began to fight for the right to lease land there. Considering the growing interest in the area, Texas Governor Ross Sterling requested the National Guard be deployed to the field to maintain order.

The finds were not all positive, though. Many people spent more than they could afford in hopes of finding oil, only to go bankrupt. There were many individuals and businesses who saw the oil fervor as a way to swindle those who didn't know much about drilling for oil. This extended to the stock markets, as the price per barrel was destabilized by new findings.

Today there are oil production facilities in over fifteen American states, but Texas is the best known for this industry because of the amount of oil it has produced. Texas continues to rely heavily on oil production for its economy.

Chapter 13 – The Space Race

One of the most quoted lines to come from Texas is the phrase "Houston, we have a problem." These words were uttered by an American astronaut who was radioing back to headquarters to try to get help in resolving a critical problem during a pivotal trip to the moon.

Houston has become one of the primary locations for the US National Aeronautics and Space Administration, or NASA. The agency was formed in response to the Soviet Union's launch of *Sputnik I,* which was the first artificial satellite to successfully reach Earth's atmosphere and orbit around the globe. The Soviet Union accomplished the successful launch of its satellite on October 4, 1957, and the US responded by passing the Space Act on July 8, 1958, and forming NASA. This was the beginning of the Space Race. Texas became instrumental in the US's efforts to achieve dominance in space.

The Formation of NASA and Its Rapid Advances

In response to the Soviet Union's satellite, the US formed NASA using existing governmental agencies, including California's Jet Propulsion Laboratory. Eisenhower and his administration feared that the Soviet Union was pulling ahead in terms of technological advances and felt it was necessary to surpass the early Soviet accomplishments.

The agency came together in October of 1958 with its primary objective to successfully launch a man into space, then return him unharmed. With its head start, the Soviet Union achieved this first when cosmonaut Yuri Gagarin reached Earth's orbit in April of 1961. The US was not far behind, though, as Alan Shepard became the first astronaut to reach space in May of 1961. He remained in the upper atmosphere for fifteen minutes. Less than a year later, in February 1962, John Glenn was the first American to enter Earth's orbit (the same feat as Gagarin).

Seeing that the Soviet Union was still about a year ahead in their technology, President John F. Kennedy announced to the US that he was initiating the Apollo Program, with the end goal of having a man walk on the moon and return unharmed.

Houston Becomes the Focus of the US Efforts in the Space Race

Before Kennedy's announcement, the beginning of the Apollo program was already underway. Knowing that they needed a dedicated facility, administrator James E. Webb began the hunt for a location to build a specialized facility, establishing the criteria that were necessary for success. The following were considered among the most vital needs for the new facilities:

1. The availability of both water transport and an advanced all-weather airport

2. A major telecommunications network near the facility

3. A large pool of potential support, including a well-established industrial economy and contractor support

4. A mild climate so that work could be conducted year-round

Houston met all these conditions and had the San Jacinto Ordnance Depot nearby. This depot offered additional benefits. For example, its military personnel had many of the important security clearances required for the NASA personnel already taken care of, and the supplies were more closely aligned with what they would need (compared to an established commercial block). There were also three prominent US universities nearby, including Rice and Texas A&M. By the end of 1962, construction on the facility was already underway. Among the first completed components were the simulations and operations so that astronauts could begin training for an experience that was largely guesswork up to that point.

The mission control center was built in Houston and has served as the major operational hub for all American space missions since Gemini IV that have required human pilots.

The Apollo Missions

Unmanned missions began in February of 1966, but the launch of humans into space had to be postponed because of the tragic accident that killed three astronauts in January 1967 as they rehearsed for the launch. Changes to the program were finally in place by October of 1968, and a new crew was selected. First, several Houston-controlled launches were conducted without any onboard pilots. Apollo 7 to 10 were all unmanned, as NASA tested and experimented with equipment.

The crew was finally launched with the goal of reaching the moon in July of 1969. Apollo 11 was on the way to deliver the first win to the US in the Space Race. On July 20th, the lunar module reached the moon, and Neil Armstrong became the first person to walk on its surface. Edwin (Buzz)Aldrin followed him a few minutes later.

The famous call to Houston occurred during the Apollo 13 mission in April of 1970. One of the oxygen tanks on the craft had exploded, damaging the craft and making it too risky for the astronauts to land on the moon. John L. (Jack) Swigert, the pilot for the command module, radioed back to the control center, saying, "Houston. We've had a problem here," which is slightly different than what is commonly quoted. He then went on to explain the problem, and against the odds, the engineers back in Houston were able to help the astronauts complete enough repairs to return to Earth. A movie based on the events was released in 1995, portraying a fraction of what the men experienced as they wondered if they would successfully return to Earth.

There were several more successful Apollo missions, up to Apollo 17. Most of them were exploratory missions in which astronauts brought back rocks and dust for further studies. The missions conducted a wide range of experiments on the moon, even hitting golf balls on the surface and driving specially-designed dune buggies. To better understand the atmosphere and environment of the moon, many of the Apollo missions conducted both solar wind experiments to see how humans would be affected and seismography measurements to determine how much of the surface could be used.

Apollo 17 was the final mission of the program, and it was completed in December of 1972. Between Apollo 11 and Apollo 17, a dozen Americans moved around on the moon, studying what was possible so far from home. Six of the missions were a success, with only Apollo 13 a failure because of the accident. The final walk on the moon occurred on December 14, 1972. The US has not sent any more astronauts to explore the moon, and no other nation has managed to achieve this singular experience.

Chapter 14 – Assassination of JFK

Although there have been many incredible events in Texas, one of the most notable in recent history was an incident that changed American history—the assassination of the 35th American President, John F. Kennedy (JFK). It has been nearly sixty years since November 22, 1963, yet the effects and legacy of that day are still ingrained in the memory of many Americans. It has also become one of the most controversial events in history, with numerous conspiracy theories formulated to explain what happened on that day in Dallas, Texas.

Preparing to Run for Re-election

As the end of 1963 neared, President John F. Kennedy was beginning to think about re-election and was in the process of starting up his campaign. His vice president was Lyndon B. Johnson, a man from Texas. During the 1960s, Texas was always politically unpredictable: they could vote for either a Democrat or a Republican for president. Knowing that Texas was a key state, it was important for Kennedy to spend some time there to persuade Texans he was still the right choice for the presidency. Though he had not yet declared that he was running for the office of president again, it was assumed that he would, and he wanted to act.

During the trip, Kennedy and his entourage traveled to nine states over the course of a week, including Texas. Ostensibly, the point of the trip was to highlight the government's efforts in managing natural resources and their conservation efforts. The real purpose, though, was to promote Kennedy as a president who focused on education, national security, and world peace. After all, he had helped to prevent a nuclear war during the Cuban Missile Crisis.

About a month after his trip around the country, Kennedy began to more openly campaign, taking a strategic approach by going to Boston and Philadelphia. He began to prepare for a lengthier strategy on November 12, 1963, and the two states that he felt were the most critical were Texas and Florida. To sway the voters, he planned to visit each state by the end of the month. The next stop on his path was Dallas, Texas. To prove that he was a family man, his wife was to accompany him to Texas. Mrs. Jacqueline Kennedy had been out of the public eye for several months after she and her husband had lost a baby in August. This was to be her first return to the campaign trail, and it was meant to be a chance to help her while supporting his political ambitions.

His presence in Texas was also meant to provide some unity within the Democratic Party, as the leaders of the party in Texas were split. In October, the United Nations Ambassador Adlai Stevenson was attacked in Dallas, so Kennedy felt his presence was needed to help calm the people of Texas, particularly in Dallas. Johnson visited just before Kennedy, essentially warming up the people of his state for the arrival of the president. Their first stop was in San Antonio, and then Houston. The president and his entourage then dined in Fort Worth with Congressman Albert Thomas to boost Thomas in the state.

November 22 and 24, 1963

The Kennedys woke in a hotel in Fort Worth. There was a steady drizzle of rain outside that did not dissuade a crowd of thousands from forming in the parking lot to see the first family. Kennedy ascended a platform and addressed the people. He talked about how strong the US was and how they were the first country in both defense and space exploration, with a strong economy that benefited the many. During this address, he had no kind of protection either from the light rain or interactions with the people.

Once his speech was over, he greeted people before heading inside for breakfast and gave another speech to the Fort Worth Chamber of Commerce. After breakfast, the procession headed to Carswell Air Force Base for a short flight to Dallas.

Upon their arrival in Dallas, both the president and the first lady addressed the people who were waiting at the fence along the exterior of the airport. They greeted individuals and thanked the people for coming out to see them. One of the well-wishers gave Mrs. Kennedy a bouquet of roses before the first family headed to meet with Governor John Connally and his wife for the trip into Dallas. The first family took the backseat in the convertible. The vice president and his wife were in a separate car in the motorcade.

After everyone was situated and ready to go, they began the ten-mile procession that went through the main streets of Dallas. The end destination was a shop where the president was to address a group of people at a luncheon. The procession slowly made its way down the streets lined with people excited to see the president and his wife. At 12:30 p.m., their car left Main Street near the Dealey Plaza and passed the Texas School Book Depository. As the procession passed the building, the sound of gunshots rang out in the air.

It is thought that three bullets were initially fired. One struck the president in the neck, and the next struck his head. The third hit the Texas governor in the back. The driver immediately sped up, heading to the Parkland Memorial Hospital that was only a few minutes from their position. Kennedy probably died as soon as he was struck by the second bullet. He was pronounced dead on arrival at the hospital, and a priest was brought in to give the nation's first Catholic president the last rites. The governor survived and eventually made a full recovery.

The president's body was loaded onto Air Force One to be taken back to Washington, DC, and on the trip, Vice President Johnson was sworn into office as president. President Kennedy was declared dead at 1 p.m. on November 22, 1963; President Johnson assumed the top position in the country at 2:38 p.m.

Lee Harvey Oswald was apprehended within two hours of the president's assassination. Two days later, on November 24, as Oswald was being transferred to the county jail, cameras were rolling as the news covered the story of the man who had killed a president. Suddenly, Jack Ruby stepped into the frame and shot Oswald in the stomach on live TV. Oswald died a few hours later at Parkland Hospital.

Aftermath

Kennedy was laid in state in the Capitol rotunda for twenty-one hours so that people could give their final farewells. An estimated 250,000 people visited during that time. Kennedy's son's farewell salute of his father's casket as it was taken to St. Matthews Cathedral was captured on film. The president was finally buried in Arlington National Cemetery a day after Oswald's death. Leaders and representatives from over 100 different countries paid their respects during the funeral.

By the end of November, President Johnson had appointed someone to investigate Kennedy's death and determine how it was possible that a president could be so easily killed. The appointee, Chief Justice Earl Warren, formed what came to be known as the Warren Commission, which was tasked with investigating the assassination of both the president and his assassin, Oswald. The commission issued its findings less than a year after the events of 1963, concluding that Oswald had acted alone. It further identified Jack Ruby as another individual who acted alone, killing Oswald out of a sense of vengeance. While less than 30% of Americans believed that Oswald had acted alone prior to the report's issuance, after the report, 87% of Americans believed there was only one assassin. This sentiment did not last long, and by 1966, people were already beginning to doubt the apparently rushed findings of the Warren Commission.

In response to rumors that the initial investigation had not had the full cooperation of all the federal agencies that were questioned, another committee was appointed to investigate the assassination in 1976. One of the findings from this second committee formed by the US House of Representatives was that there was almost certainly a second gunman—they did not think that Oswald had acted alone. This conclusion was based on a transmission tape that they had retrieved from Dallas that included evidence of at least four shots, perhaps more. This generated a lot of attention, and acoustic experts were called in to verify the sounds to see if the finding was accurate. According to the experts, the recording was too degraded to determine how many shots were fired; the tape was worthless. The same committee also investigated the assassination of Dr. Martin Luther King, Jr.

The Kennedy assassination not only revealed problems in how easy it was to gain access to the president but also put a spotlight on Texas and its response to the tragedy. While a lot of attention went to the Warren Commission, both the Texas attorney general and the Department of Public Safety initiated their own investigations into the events leading up to the assassination. Texas could be criticized not only for failing to protect the president but also for failing to secure the safety of the assassin.

A Wealth of Conspiracies

The assassination of John F. Kennedy has drawn a lot of attention, becoming a popular source for conspiracy theories. These theories only worsened following the re-opening of the investigation and the declaration that there was more than one assassin present that day, even after auditory experts discredited the tape. People have pointed to a wide range of evidence, such as scrapes in the concrete that were said to have hurt one of the people watching the procession, something that would not have been possible for Oswald to do. The initial disbelief that a single person could kill the president continues, and there is plenty of criticism of both the way local Texas officials and federal agencies had left many gaps in security. Americans have been coming up with many different explanations for what happened that day in 1963, from conspiracies claiming that the US government killed him, to speculation that the vice president was behind it (Kennedy was killed in Johnson's home state), to theories about aliens. It has become a favorite popular reference for TV, movies, and stories because of the amount of uncertainty that surrounds exactly what happened that day.

Chapter 15 – Texas Today

With its rich and varied history, Texas has evolved into a completely unique state within the US. It attracts millions of tourists every year seeking to learn the history of Texas, experience the Wild West in a much safer environment, and explore lands that were traveled by some of the most notable names in history.

Basic Texas Statistics

From a small group of settlements and large regions of indigenous people to the 28th state in the US to the center of the American effort in the Space Race, the evolution of Texas has made for some very singular statistics and a very diverse population. There are nearly 1,000 miles (1,600 km) between the northern and southern tip of the state and roughly the same distance between the east and the furthermost western side. Most of the state's boundaries are currently defined by bodies of water, including the Gulf of Mexico to the southeast and rivers that divide Texas from Oklahoma, Louisiana, and Arkansas. The Rio Grande is a large and beautiful border that divides a large portion of Texas and Mexico.

The state capital is still Austin, named for the first American to successfully establish an American settlement in the state. Today, Stephen Austin is known as the Father of Texas. Houston has the largest population in the state, and other major cities include Dallas,

Fort Worth, and San Antonio. Dallas, Houston, and San Antonio all rank in the ten most populated cities in the US.

With the state becoming a hub for NASA, other technological industries have established footholds there, as well. The employment these industries represent has drawn a steady influx of people to Texas, and it is often one of the states with the largest population growth in the country. Starting in the 1970s, these trends have helped to change the state's demographics.

Texas's Evolving Economy and Education

Initially, Texas settlers prospered from farming and ranching. Following reconstruction, the state's economy became much more diverse, in large part because the Union began to try to modernize the south. Had the South had many of the economic benefits they gained after the war, they would have had a better chance of success. Before the Civil War, southern states primarily relied on slavery to prosper, as their economies were all based on farming and ranching. However, the economies did not entirely change; rather, the states expanded as they tried to learn how to work without slaves to support them. Cattle, cotton, and oil are all still primary sources of revenue for Texas, but the state has seen understandable growth in technology, banking, insurance, and construction as it has prospered over the last century.

There are over 140 colleges and universities in Texas, including community and junior colleges. The University of Texas, located in Austin, has about 50,000 students a year. Both the University of Texas and Texas A&M University have internationally-recognized graduate programs that attract people from around the globe every year. The prestigious private Rice University, located in Houston, produces graduates that meet higher than average academic standards.

Terrain and Climates

Texas can be divided into seven primary regions: Panhandle Plains, Big Bend, Hill Country, Prairies & Lakes, Piney Woods, South Texas Plains, and the Gulf Coast.

Coupled with its history, the diverse climate of Texas makes it an ideal place for visitors.

Texas Drought

While most people think of Texas as an expansive desert, it has a rich history of ranches and farming. During the early part of the 21st century, the state experienced serious droughts that are forcing ranchers to request assistance and look for innovative ways to take care of their cattle. Twenty-five percent of the population live in drought areas, with another 21% in abnormally dry areas. The southern regions of the state are the most adversely affected, and as late as 2020, there were many sites dedicated to monitoring the weather and temperatures to provide as much notification to ranchers as possible.

Conclusion

While all the states in the US have their own stories and histories, there is no history quite as singular as that of Texas. There is a reason why it is known as the "Lone Star State."

It is the only state that was once its own country and only became a country because the US would not annex it (Hawaii was its own country before US businessmen overthrew the Hawaiian monarchy, but up to that point, no nation claimed Hawaii as its own). Though most people are aware of the state's history as a stand-alone country, many are unaware of the time before this, and even less is known about the period before the arrival of Spain in the Western Hemisphere.

Texas is one of the few states that has seen an interesting mix of different demographics because of its pivotal role in the European exploration of North America. Initially, it was of little interest to the Spanish explorers as they learned that North America did not have the riches that they had found in South and Central America. Missionaries went out to try to convert the native peoples, and soldiers joined them to establish settlements, but that did not last long. France posed a threat to the Spanish claim, which was what drove the Spaniards to try to establish settlements. However, the Spanish were not accustomed to creating settlements from scratch, and this reduced their odds of success. As the territory became increasingly less stable and profitable, Spain began to look for ways to get more money from the region, even as they tried to control the growing resentment against them in Mexico City and around the colony. As Spain invited Americans to move to the region of Tejas, Mexico was waging a war for its own independence. By the time the first American settlers were ready to make the move to Texas, Spain was no longer in control of Mexico.

Mexico decided to continue the attempt to turn the northern regions into profitable settlements, so they made agreements like the ones that Spain had made with the Americans. The conditions were similar, but Mexico could not do much to ensure the settlers lived up to their end of the agreement. Relying on the leaders of the settlements resulted in growing resentment when Mexico tried to force the settlers to honor the agreements they had made. The fact that Mexico was slow to find its feet and civil war within Mexico quickly followed the end of the War for Mexican Independence revealed a weakness. When the settlers saw it, they started the War for Texas Independence, with the hope that the US would provide support and annex them into the country.

The Texans won their independence, but the US was hesitant to annex the small nation, knowing that the Mexicans would view it negatively. That sentiment changed about ten years later when the US president decided he wanted to realize the growing belief in Manifest Destiny. After the Mexican-American War, the desire for statehood was finally realized, but Texas would quickly learn that it should have remained its own country.

About fifteen years after becoming the 28th state, Texas joined the Confederates in seceding from the US. The Civil War and Reconstruction proved to be particularly trying times in Texas history, but with the help of the US government, the state was put on a path that would eventually lead to a much more diverse economy, with industries other than plantations and ranching. The state began to play a significant role in the US during the 20th century. From the establishment of the NASA main control center in Houston to the assassination of President Kennedy, Texas has continued to have a history that is completely unique.

Here's another book by Captivating History
that you might be interested in

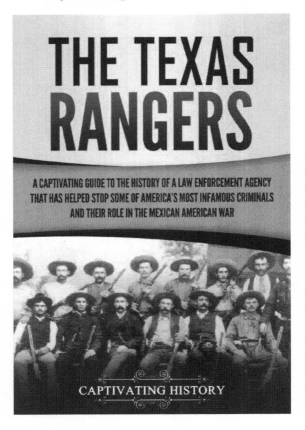

Free Bonus from Captivating History (Available for a Limited time)

Hi History Lovers!

Now you have a chance to join our exclusive history list so you can get your first history ebook for free as well as discounts and a potential to get more history books for free! Simply visit the link below to join.

Captivatinghistory.com/ebook

Also, make sure to follow us on Facebook, Twitter and Youtube by searching for Captivating History.

Bibliography

"Remember the Alamo!," 1836, EyeWitness to History, 2020, Ibis
Communications Inc, www.eyewitnesstohistory.com/

2. Imperial Rivalry II: Spain & France in Tejas (Texas), National Humanities
Center, 2020, nationalhumanitiescenter.org/

29d. The Mexican-American War, US History, 2019, Independent Hall
Association in Philadelphia, www.ushistory.org/

A Brief History of the Texas Rangers, Mike Cox, 2018, Texas Ranger Hall of Fame
and Museum, www.texasranger.org/

Alamo: Monument, San Antonio, Texas, United States, The Editors of
Encyclopedia Britannica, 2020, www.britannica.com/

American Indians; A Story Told for Thousands of Years, Bullock Texas State
History Museum, 2020, www.thestoryoftexas.com/

Anglo-American Colonization Efforts, Texas State Library, 2020, Archives
Commissions, www.tsl.texas.gov/

Anglo-American Colonization, Margaret Swett Henson, 2020, Texas State
Historical Association, tshaonline.org/

Apache Indians, Jeffrey D. Carlisle, 2020, Texas State Historical
Association, tshaonline.org/

Apollo: Space Program, The Editors of Encyclopedia Britannica,
2020, www.britannica.com/

Causes of Texas Independence, Christopher Minster, May 30, 2019, Thought
Co., www.thoughtco.com/

Civil War, Ralph A. Wooster, Brett J. Derbes, 2020, Texas State Historical
Association, tshaonline.org/

Conquistadors, Bullock Texas State History Museum,
2020, www.thestoryoftexas.com/

Father of Texan Independence, Christopher Minister, July 21, 2019, Thought
Co., www.thoughtco.com/

First Oil Discoveries, America Oil & Gas Historical Society, 2020, aoghs.org/

First Texas Oil Boom, Petroleum Pioneers, 2020, American Oil & Gas Historical Society, aoghs.org/

Fredonian Rebellion, Archie P. McDonald, 2020, Texas State Historical Association, tshaonline.org/

French-Spanish Rivalry in Tejas (Texas), 1685-1690), National Humanities Center, 2020, nationalhumanitiescenter.org/

Gonzales, Battle of, Stephen L. Hardin, 2020, Texas State Historical Association, tshaonline.org/

History of Johnson Space Center, NASA, August 3, 2017, www.nasa.gov/

History of Oil Discoveries in Texas, Texas Almanac, 2020, Texas State Historical Association, texasalmanac.com/

Houston, We've Had a Problem, James A. Lovell, 2020, Apollo Expeditions to the Moon, history.nasa.gov/

Independence and Revolution, 2020, Mexico Newsletter, Mexperience, www.mexperience.com

Joint Resolution for Annexing Texas to the United States Approved March 1, 1845, Peters, Richard, August 24, 2011, Texas State Library, www.tsl.texas.gov/

Los Diablos Tejanos, Michal Gray, 2000, Images of the West, www.imageswest.digitalimagepro.com/

Mexican Rule – 1821 – 1835, Katie Whitehurst, 2020, Historical Eras, Texas Our Texas, texasourtexas.texaspbs.org/

Mexican Rule – 1821 – 1835, Katie Whitehurst, 2020, Historical Eras, Texas Our Texas, texasourtexas.texaspbs.org/

Mexican Texas, Arando De Léon, 2020, Texas State Historical Association, tshaonline.org/

Mexican-American War (1846-48), US Navy, August 19, 2019, Naval History and Heritage Command, www.history.navy.mil/

Narrative History of Texas Annexation, Jean Carefoot, August 24, 2011, Texas State Library, www.tsl.texas.gov/

November 22, 1963: Death of the President, John F. Kennedy President Library and Museum, 2020, National Archives, www.jfklibrary.org/

Reconstruction, Carl M. Moneyhon, 2020, Texas State Historical Association, tshaonline.org/

Remembering the Alamo, Bruce Selcraig, April 1, 2004, Smithsonian Magazine, www.smithsonianmag.com/

Spanish Colonial 1689-1821, Katie Whitehurst, 2020, PBS, texasourtexas.texaspbs.org/

Spanish Colonial, Katie Whitehurst, 2020, PBS, texasourtexas.texaspbs.org/

Stephen Fuller Austin, PBS, 2001, New Perspectives on The West, www.pbs.org/

Texas During the Civil War, Louis J. Wortham, 2020, Texas Military Forces Museum, www.texasmilitaryforcesmuseum.org/

Texas Rangers, Bullock Museum, 2020, Bullock Texas State History Museum, www.thestoryoftexas.com/

Texas Revolution, Jeff Wallenfeldt, 2020, Encyclopedia Britannica Inc, www.britannica.com/

Texas: State, United States, Gregory Lewis McNamee, DeWitt C. Reddick, Ralph A. Wooster, January 17, 2020, Encyclopedia Britannica, www.britannica.com/

The Apollo Mission, NASA, February 1, 2019, www.nasa.gov/

The Comanche – Horsemen of the Plains, Legends of America, 2020, www.legendsofamerica.com/

The Mexican American War, PBS, 2020, American Experience, www.pbs.org/

The Mexican-American War in a Nutshell, NCC staff, May 13, 2019, Constitution Daily, National Constitution Center, constitutioncenter.org/

The Republic for Texas – The Texas Revolution Texas Declaration of Independence, Texas State Library, 2020, www.tsl.texas.gov/

The Spanish Colonial Era in Texas, study.com, 2020, study.com/

The Start of the Space Race, Khan Academy, 2020, www.khanacademy.org/

The Texas Revolutionary War (1835-1836), 2020, United States History, www.uswars.net/

Three Shots Fired at President Kennedy's Motorcade..., Texas State Library, 2020, www.tsl.texas.gov/

Why the Public Stopped Believing the Government about JFK's Murder, Steve M. Gillon, November 21, 2019, History, A&E Television Networks, www.history.com/

Made in the USA
Coppell, TX
06 March 2024

29829225R00067